Second Congregation Belfast 1708–2008

Roger Courtney

Foreword by William Crawley

THE AUTHOR

Dr Roger Courtney was born and brought up in a liberal Presbyterian family in Belfast. He was the founder of Crescent Arts Centre in Belfast, then the Chief Executive of the Simon Community, working with people who are homeless for sixteen years, for which he was awarded an MBE. Since then he has been a freelance advisor to a wide range of voluntary organisations and has published several books on voluntary sector management. He has been closely involved in the reconciliation work of the Corrymeela Community. He is a song and hymn writer. His peace anthem, *The Pollen of Peace*, has been translated into six languages and is sung around the world. He is currently researching and writing a book on the progressive tradition within Irish Presbyterianism.

ACKNOWLEDGEMENTS

I am very grateful to: Rev. Chris Hudson for helping me find a spiritual home and suggesting I write this short history for the Tercentenary of Second congregation Belfast; Rev. Tom Banham for helpful advice in tracking down useful materials in the First Belfast library; Rev. John Nelson, writer of Dry as Dust in The Non-Subscribing Presbyterian, for allowing me to draw on his research for Dry as Dust and commenting on two earlier drafts; Jim Jackson for helping me to navigate the various materials around All Souls', showing me the joys of Adobe Photoshop in preparing the illustrations and photographs for publication and for interviewing Ruby Purdy; Ruby Purdy for sharing her memories of York Street congregation's move to All Souls'; Rev W McMillan, Charlie Stewart and Isabella Evangelisti for commenting on an earlier draft and to my family, Christine, Emma, Carol and Cal for their love and forbearance.

Published in 2008 by All Souls' Non-Subscribing Presbyterian congregation

CONTENTS

Page

PROFILES

SPECIAL FEATURES

ILLUSTRATIONS

The front cover is based on a watercolour of All Souls' by David Evans. The illustrations in pages 1–63 are taken from S. Shannon Millin's 1900 "A History of Second Congregation Belfast". The remaining illustrations were provided by members of the congregation, or are taken from the church archives.

Illustrations and photographs of individuals:

FOREWORD

The story of Second Congregation is the story of Belfast.
Many of the most significant and colourful personalities in
the development of Belfast as a newly important merchant
town in the 18th century are encountered in the pages of
this history.

Belfast was also a centre of radical ideas in politics and
in religion; and Second Congregation's story is also a
fascinating account of a dissenting, free-thinking,
intellectually challenging tradition within Irish
Presbyterianism.

Roger Courtney's history reveals a community that was,
from its earliest days, open to new ideas: a 'new light'
fellowship of men and women who prized liberty of
conscience and campaigned for a more equal society.
Democratic values shaped their politics and their theology,
as did an unflinching commitment to the possibility of
human progress.

A former minister of Second Congregation, the Reverend
William Hamilton Drummond (1778–1865), in some
ways embodies the adventurousness and creativity of
this community's distinctive approach to life: he was a
theologian and poet, an educationalist and political radical,
and an early advocate of the rights of animals. Surprisingly
modern ideas have always found been welcomed – then
interrogated – in the radical tradition to which Second
Congregation belongs.

Belfast today is a post-conflict city re-negotiating its place
in the world. Its growing population is ethnically and
religiously diverse; where once it was associated with
bombs, it is now increasingly associated with building sites

and peace processes. This is the changing context in which Second Congregation, now known as All Souls', finds itself. And Roger Courtney's history is evidence that few congregations are as richly equipped historically to address the postmodern challenges of the new Belfast as All Souls'.

WILLIAM CRAWLEY

WILLIAM CRAWLEY is a BBC journalist and broadcaster with the BBC. His radio and TV credits range from the weekly Sunday Sequence programme for BBC Radio Ulster, which explores religion, ethics and cultural ideas, to the three-part Blueprint TV series, which examines 600 million years of Ireland's natural history. He also regularly presents news and current affairs progammes on Radio Ulster, and arts programmes for BBC Radio 3. Educated in Belfast, Northern Ireland, and Princeton, New Jersey, he is a former Presbyterian chaplain to the University of Ulster.

INTRODUCTION

The following is a short history of the Second
Congregation, Belfast, now known as All Souls'. It has
its roots in Rosemary Street Belfast three hundred years
ago, where it grew out of First Belfast congregation in a
rapidly expanding Belfast. It moved to Elmwood Avenue
at the end of the Nineteenth Century. In the Twentieth
Century it was joined by the congregation of York Street
Non-Subscribing Presbyterian Church, whose building
had been destroyed during WWII, to create the present
All Souls' Church (combining Second Belfast and York
Street Non-Subscribing Presbyterian congregations).

1

The history is structured into seven chapters. The first considers why religious freedom has become a crucial touchstone for the congregation over three hundred years. The second explores the early development of Presbyterianism in Ireland in the 17th Century. The third looks particularly at the establishment and early development of the Second congregation in Rosemary Street (1708–1895). The fourth highlights the building of All Souls' Church in Elmwood Avenue and the congregation's life in it's new home (1895–1941). The fifth takes us on a slight detour to look at the establishment and development of the York Street congregation (1833–1941), up to its destruction in the Blitz. The sixth then looks at the life of All Souls' as a combined church with both congregations (Second Belfast and York Street). The seventh and final chapter considers what the future might hold.

Interspersed within the historical narrative are 22 profiles of particular individuals who have been particularly associated with Second Belfast and York Street congregations. These include ministers and lay members who had made a significant contribution to the religious, civic or cultural life of Belfast, and sometimes, further afield.

There are also two special features: one on the prayer book tradition in Second congregation; and the other on the Domestic Mission established jointly by First and Second congregations.

THE STRUGGLE FOR RELIGIOUS FREEDOM

At the back of All Souls' church in Elmwood Avenue, on a tablet "to commemorate the loyalty of the congregation to the principles of religious liberty", erected on the bi-centenary of Second congregation, is the following quotation from 2 Corinthians 3:17:

Where the Sprit of the Lord is there is Liberty

This commitment to the concept of religious freedom has been the touchstone of Second congregation for three hundred years. Below, is outlined how the Non-Subscribing

3

Presbyterian tradition grew out of centuries of struggle for religious freedom, before looking in more detail at the specific history of the Second congregation. Five key stages in this struggle are relevant here:

Firstly, when on Halloween 1517, Augustinian monk Martin Luther tacked his 95 Theses on the church door in Wittenberg, Germany, attacking the corrupt practices of the Catholic church at that time, he started what would become known as the Reformation and the creation of Protestant churches which were free from allegiance to the worldwide church centred on Rome. However, in most of these churches, the idea of a confessional state where the political, legal and religious hierarchy, from the monarch, as head of the church, down, remained completely intertwined. The basis for beliefs became the Bible, which everyone, not just the clergy, could read and interpret. With Protestants there was to be no mediator between God and the people.

Secondly, the reforms of John Calvin and Theodore Beza in Switzerland, Thomas Cartwright in England and, crucially for Ulster, John Knox in Scotland, resulted in a fundamental shake-up in church structures, where a top-down hierarchy was replaced with a bottom-up democracy. Decisions in individual congregations became the responsibility of the church session made up of elders of the congregation. The word Presbyterian means simply that oversight of the churches affairs is by a Presbytery or council not an Episcopal hierarchy.

Thirdly, Scottish Presbyterians faced periods of both religious and political persecution, as well as economic hardship. The religious and political establishment tried hard to maintain a confessional state in Scotland, based on the Episcopal hierarchy, and in 1610 even managed to re-establish it for a short time. Many Scottish Presbyterian tenant farmers moved to Ulster to escape from this oppression.

Fourthly, during the late eighteenth century in Ireland, many Presbyterians led the United Irishmen's campaign in Ulster against the Confessional State, controlled by the Episcopal church, which continued to perpetuate oppressive political, legal and religious authority and oppress both Roman Catholic and Dissenting traditions. For much of the century Presbyterians were largely unable to get appointments to official civil, legal, political or military offices; Presbyterian ordination (until 1719) was not legally recognised; and marriages by Presbyterian ministers were considered to be invalid. Combined with severe economic injustice, this explosive mix resulted in the Rebellion of 1798. Although it was easily suppressed, over the following century, nearly all the original grievances of the Dissenters were eventually addressed.

Fifthly, from the founding of the Presbyterian Church, there had been debates about the precise theological basis of Presbyterianism. In 1646 a group of English Dissenters came together in Westminster, London to create both a structure for the Presbyterian church and a statement of its faith, entitled *The Confession of Faith; the larger and shorter catechisms, with the scripture proofs at large; together with the sum of saving knowledge, (contained in the Holy Scriptures, and held forth in the said confession and catechisms,) and practical use thereof.* This became known as the Westminster Confession of Faith and while English Presbyterianism had limited impact, in Scotland, despite a setback in 1610, the Presbyterian Church of Scotland adopted the Confession and became the dominant denomination there.

With the development of Presbyterianism in Ireland it became an issue of regular controversy as to whether unambiguous subscription to the Confession should be compulsory for ministers, students for the ministry and church elders. Those in favour of religious freedom, who opposed subscription, argued, and still argue, that Scripture

5

is the fundamental basis of the Presbyterian faith, not a doctrinal statement created by men and therefore individual conscience should allow individuals to interpret the Scriptures as they see fit. The ministers of both First and Second Presbyterian Church Belfast were of "New Light" or "Latitudinarian" (there should be latitude to interpret the Scriptures according to individual conscience) views and so opposed compulsory subscription. The argument continued through the eighteenth century and resulted in the creation of the Presbytery of Antrim for Non-Subscribing congregations, and then in the nineteenth century seventeen congregations, also opposed to compulsory Subscription, seceded from the General Synod of Ulster and formed the Remonstrant Synod of Ulster. The congregations within the Presbytery of Antrim and Remonstrant Synod eventually came together with other Non-Subscribing bodies and the Synod of Ulster to form the Non-Subscribing Presbyterian Church of Ireland.

So, with a history of these struggles for religious, civil and political freedom, it is clear how religious freedom became the core theme or motif of the Non-Subscribing Church in Ireland and one that its members hold dear.

THE DEVELOPMENT OF IRISH
PRESBYTERIANISM IN THE 17th CENTURY

With the plantation of Ulster came Presbyterians from
Scotland and, to a lesser extent, from England. In the main
these were not landowners, but tenant farmers, many of
whom were escaping from persecution and economic
hardship. Along with these migrants came a small number
of Presbyterian ministers, particularly from Scotland.
Initially the Episcopal Church welcomed these ministers,
because they helped fill vacancies in churches in Ireland. In
1613 Edward Bryce became the first Presbyterian minister
in Ireland. However, in 1634 the Episcopal Church decided
to enforce religious conformity. As they no longer wanted

The illustration above is of Second Church in Rosemary Street Belfast

7

these non-conforming dissenters as ministers, they were evicted from the churches and their livings. Presbyterian services were made illegal, as were Presbyterian marriages and funerals. Many ministers returned to Scotland. Those who remained in Ulster were forced to preach in secret, in barns or fields, often suffering great hardships and harassment from the authorities, who wielded a combination of political, legal and religious power in Ireland. Some Presbyterians tried to emigrate on the *Eagle Wing*, but after a month at sea bad weather forced them to return.

When a Scottish army was sent by the King to quell the rebellion of 1641 that the native Irish population had hoped would expel the English and Scottish settlers and enable them to return to their lands, many Scottish Presbyterians and their chaplains came to Ireland as part of the army and some chose to remain after the rebellion was put down. This provided a significant boost to the fledgling church, which began to formalise itself. The first Presbytery in Ireland was formed in 1642 by the Army chaplains and officers as Presbyterian elders in Carrickfergus. Three years later the First Presbyterian Church, in the small town of Belfast, was established in Rosemary Street. Its first minister was Rev. John Baird, followed by Rev. Anthony Shaw.

In January 1649 King Charles was executed. The Presbytery met in Belfast two weeks later and drew up a "representation" condemning the execution, which they ordered to be read from every Presbyterian pulpit. In 1653 Cromwell assumed power as Lord Protector. Presbyterianism, although officially proscribed, was tolerated and received a state grant. Cromwell died in 1658 and two years later Charles II was invited to return to his father's throne. The grant ended and persecutions of Presbyterians were renewed, in an effort to make them conform to the Established Church.

The loyalty of Presbyterians was further questioned when, in 1663, "Blood's Plot" led by Presbyterian minister, Rev. William Lecky, resulted in over forty Presbyterian ministers being detained on suspicion of involvement. Lecky was executed. The following year four Presbyterian ministers were excommunicated and imprisoned for six years for refusing to conform to the Established Church. The establishment continued to look on Presbyterians with great suspicion.

In 1672 Charles II issued a Declaration of Indulgence enabling Catholics and Presbyterians to worship freely and the regium donum given to Presbyterian ministers was granted for the first time. The Established Church continued to use every opportunity to oppress dissenting Presbyterians. Four ministers were jailed for almost a year for proclaiming a fast. In 1685 Charles died and was succeeded by his Catholic brother, James II. Catholics were appointed to public position including to that of the Viceroy. James II issued his own Declaration of Liberty of Conscience permitting all citizens to profess any religion.

William of Orange was invited to invade England in 1688 and chase out his father-in-law James. James then landed in Kinsale and the conflict between him and William took place in Ireland, including the siege of Derry and the Battle of the Boyne, where James was defeated. Terms were agreed by the Treaty of Limerick. William rewarded the loyalty of Irish Presbyterians, who could easily have taken sides against the hated Episcopal establishment, with the renewal of the regium donum grant and the Presbyterian Synod was able to meet in the open. There was a new wave of migration of Scottish Presbyterians to Ulster. The Established Church bishops and landlords used their control of the Irish parliament to prevent the passing of toleration bills to improve the legal position of Presbyterians and a pamphlet war took place between the Established Church and the Presbyterians.

9

In May 1691, Thomas Emlin, who was born in Stamford, Lincolnshire, England in 1663, accepted a call from Wood Street Church in Dublin and was a minister there for eleven years. He was considered to be of great ability and an eminent preacher. In 1702, however, Dr. Duncan Cumyng, a member of the congregation, told the senior minister, Rev. Joseph Boyse, that he had doubts about Emlin's orthodoxy, because of his failure to ever mention the concept of the Trinity in sermons or prayers. Emlin was questioned and made it clear that he did not believe that Christ was equal to God and called into question the doctrine of the Trinity. Boyse, while theologically orthodox, was a leading supporter of non-subscription to the Westminster Confession of Faith. However he was concerned about Emlin's heterodoxy in regard to the deity of Christ. Emlin was eventually removed from his ministry by the other Dublin Presbyterian ministers on the instigation of Boyse, because of his unorthodox views, particularly on the Trinity. Boyse and Emlin continued the argument about the nature of the Trinity by pamphlet. As a result of one of these pamphlets, Emlin, on a visit to Dublin to settle his affairs in 1703 was charged and convicted of blasphemy by a court, including the Archbishops of Armagh and Dublin and five Bishops. He was forced to walk round the forecourt with a placard around his neck proclaiming his offence, was imprisoned for two years, fined £1,000, and disowned by his friends and fellow clergy. Emlin's conviction also had consequences in Ulster, where it gave ammunition to the orthodox subscribers to demand that all Presbyterian ministers be required to sign the Westminster Confession of Faith. He died in London in 1741.

David Buttle (sometimes spelt Butle), a Belfast merchant, Burgess of Belfast from 1700 and Sovereign of Belfast from 1702 to 1704, was originally a member of First Belfast congregation who then became a member of the new Second congregation, under Rev. James Kirkpatrick.

In 1698 the Dublin Parliament passed an *Act to Prevent the Further Growth of Popery*, requiring all those in official public positions to *"receive the sacrament of the Lord's Supper, according to the rites and usages of the Established Church"*, thereby effectively excluding any non-conformists and Dissenters, as well as Catholics. Buttle, William Crawford (also spelt Craford), John Chalmers, Edward Brice and Neile McNeile were all expelled from Belfast Corporation, which caused huge consternation and resentment amongst the Presbyterian community. Large numbers of Presbyterians decided to emigrate during this period.

In 1698 the Synod of Ulster decided to make subscription to the Westminster Confession of Faith (see above), which had been drawn up in London in 1646, obligatory for students to the Presbyterian ministry. This was the first shot in a conflict between those "new light" latitudinarians, or non-subscribers, who believed that the Bible and individual conscience were the ultimate authority and, therefore, no other theological creed should be imposed, and those who wished to impose the Westminster Confession of Faith on ministers, students and elders. This dispute would continue to disturb the Presbyterian Church for the next one hundred and fifty years.

Rev. James Kirkpatrick

Some well known individuals associated with the Second congregation

Rev James Kirkpatrick*
(c.1676–c.1743)

James Kirkpatrick was born in either Ireland or Scotland around 1676. He was the son of Rev. Hugh Kirkpatrick who was a Presbyterian minister in Lurgan and Ballymoney in Ireland and Old Cumnock in Scotland.

James Kirkpatrick graduated in theology from the University of Glasgow where his fellow students included John Abernethy and John Simson (who, as a professor in the University, would be accused of heresy). Kirkpatrick was licensed by Route Presbytery in 1697/8 and was ordained in Templepatrick, County Antrim on 7 August 1699, where he served as minister from 1699 to 1706. In 1706 he was appointed to be the assistant to Rev. John McBride in First Belfast. The church expanded to such an extent that, in 1708, a Second church was built in Rosemary Street and Kirkpatrick became its minister. In 1712 he was elected Moderator of the Irish Presbyterian church.

Kirkpatrick was a leading member of the Belfast Society, with Rev. Abernethy, minister in Antrim, who had studied with him in Glasgow under Simson and kept in touch. The Society was established in 1705 for dissenting ministers, elders and students for the ministry to discuss ideas, including social and theological issues. Although an orthodox Trinitarian, Kirkpatrick was one of a group of ministers who tried to persuade the church that it should not require its ministers to subscribe to the Westminster Confession of Faith. He wrote a pamphlet in defence of non-subscription, which was published under the name of one of the elders in his church, Dr Victor Ferguson, an ancestor of Sarah Ferguson, the Duchess of York and it became known as *Ferguson's Vindication*.

Not only was Kirkpatrick a minister, but also a qualified doctor, a profession which he practiced towards the end of his life. He wrote several works outlining his theological position, including, *A Vindication of the Presbyterian Ministers in the North of Ireland*, which indicates how broad his views of religious liberty were, and *A Defence of Christian Liberty*. The exact date and place of his death and burial are unknown, although he died while he was writing "*The Defence of Christian Liberty*" around 1743/4.

* Sources: Bradbury 2002; Holmes 1985; Brooke 1994; Kilroy 1994; McBride 1998; Stewart 1993; Witherow 1858; Herlihy 1998.

13

SECOND CONGREGATION ROSEMARY STREET
1708–1895

Ireland at the beginning of the eighteenth century continued to be a difficult place to be Presbyterian, in relation to marriage, funerals, education, wills and tithes, swinging from reluctant toleration to severe repression. William Crawford (Craford), a merchant and printer, who helped establish the Second congregation, was a burgess and sovereign of Belfast until 1707 when he was removed for being a dissenter. He was, however, a member of parliament from 1703 to 1713.

In 1706 James Kirkpatrick (see profile), minister of Templepatrick, was called to First Belfast Congregation to

---

The illustration is of the interior of Second Church Rosemary Street Belfast

14

be assistant to John McBride, who had fled to Scotland to avoid being arrested for refusing to take an oath abjuring the claims to the throne of James II's son. Kirkpatrick was a member of the Belfast Society which had been formed a year earlier to provide Presbyterian ministers, elders and students with progressive "new light" views with an open forum for debate on theological and other issues.

By 1707 the First Belfast congregation had grown substantially with the expansion of the town of Belfast and increasing numbers of Scots settling in Ulster. They were looking at the prospect of having over 3,000 members of the congregation. To accommodate this expansion, when Rev. McBride returned from Scotland, it was agreed to divide the congregation between the existing (First) and a new church (Second), despite the opposition of many in the original congregation. The new church was built just behind the existing one in Rosemary Street (unfortunately no representation of the original church exists). The theology of both churches was "New Light" and therefore opposed to compulsory subscription to the Westminster Confession of Faith.

In 1708 Rev. James Kirkpatrick was appointed as the minister of the new Second congregation in Rosemary Street Belfast, and remained as minister until 1743. He wrote various publications, including *A Historical Essay on the Loyalty of Presbyterians in Great Britain from the Reformation to this Present Year 1713*, (to which David Buttle and others attached their names), which outlined the sacrifices made by Presbyterians in Ireland and the persecutions that they had inflicted on them. He attempted in detail to justify Presbyterian loyalty to the king, while retaining the right to oppose his laws and the established church and argued for the importance of individual conscience. He made it clear that loyalty was not synonymous with conformity to the established church,

If we once believe that their consciences truly
dictated to them the points wherein they differed
from the Established Church, they could not
(without manifest contempt of the authority of
God) forbear to put their principles in practice.

For Kirkpatrick, Presbyterianism encouraged individual
self-reliance in opposition to authority in both Church and
State,

The ecclesiastical constitution of presbytery
does provide such effectual remedies against the
usurpation and ambition of the clergy, and lays
such foundations for the liberty of the individual
in church matters, that it naturally creates in the
people an aversion from all tyranny and
oppression in the state also.

The attempt by the Established Church to maintain
complete religious, civil and military control continued
with the passing of the Schism Act of 1714 which made it
illegal to be a teacher or tutor unless you were a member
of the Established Church of England.

In 1718 First congregation called the controversial "New
Light" minister John Abernethy, the Presbyterian minister
in Antrim, but Synod refused to sanction the move, so the
following year the congregation called Samuel Haliday as
their minister. Haliday had been educated in the universities
of Glasgow and Leiden, Holland. He was a vocal supporter
of the non-subscribers and was accused of being an Arian
(who were accused of not accepting the full divinity of
Christ) – an accusation he refuted. At his installation in
1720 he refused to subscribe to the Westminster Confession
of Faith and the four other ministers attending protested
against continuing with the installation, but were over-ruled
by minister of Second congregation, Kirkpatrick, who was
acting as Moderator at the installation.

In 1720, to try and reduce the conflict over subscription to the Westminster Confession of Faith, Synod passed the Pacific Act, which allowed ministers to state reservations to Confession when they signed it. Despite objections, however, Synod continued to insist on subscription to the Westminster Confession. In 1721 it invited all Presbyterian ministers to renew their subscription, as a way of flushing out those whose theological views were considered to be unorthodox. The ministers of First and Second congregations still did not subscribe. Because of this some of the more orthodox members of Kirkpatrick's Second and Haliday's First congregations left to form the Third Belfast Congregation, creating yet another Presbyterian church in Rosemary Street, with financial support from Calvinist Scottish Presbyterians. Its first minister was Rev. Charles Masterson, previously minister of Connor, County Antrim.

At the first communion service in the new Third Presbyterian Church in 1724, both Haliday and Kirkpatrick were excluded because of their perceived views and refusal to subscribe to the Westminster Confession. This obviously angered the two ministers and Kirkpatrick responded by writing a pamphlet, *A Scripture plea against a fatal rupture and breach of Christian communion.*

In 1727, although most congregations in Ulster remained united, several divided in two on the issue of subscription, including Dromore and Newtownards. The tide seemed to be increasingly turning against the non-subscribers. To try and deal with this rift in the church, the Non-Subscribing congregations were, by a narrow majority, placed into one presbytery – the Presbytery of Antrim, although there was no particular geographical connection with Antrim. Non-Subscribing ministers were still recognised as Presbyterian ministers and could be called to churches in other Presbyteries, but they could not vote at the General Synod. Kirkpatrick, who had substantial support from the expanding wealthy and educated urban classes in Belfast, complained,

> *Nothing is more common amongst poor Country-people and amongst all who are ignorant of the state of the controversy, than to vent their jealousies against the Non-Subscribers, and to say plainly that there must be something at the bottom of their Non-Subscribing more than what has come to light; and by this means, all the ministers who have subscribed are teaz'd for their charity and Christian Forbearance toward their dear Brethren.*

By 1726 Rev. Kirkpatrick of Second congregation and twelve other ministers and their congregations (Antrim, Ballyclare, Duneane, Ahogill, Larne, Cairncastle, Holywood, First Belfast, Moira, Newtownards and Aghadowey) had been formed into the Presbytery of Antrim, which did not require subscription. Kirkpatrick tried to heal the rift within Presbyterianism by writing *Expedients for peace among the Protestant Dissenters in the North of Ireland,* but was rebuffed.

The Presbyterian Church had always insisted that its students should be educated to degree level. With the absence of any higher education college or university in Ireland that admitted Presbyterians, most students for the ministry went to Glasgow University. In 1729, Francis Hutcheson, a "new light" Presbyterian minister and one of Ireland's greatest philosophers became Professor of Moral Philosophy in Glasgow. Not only would his progressive utilitarian views have a profound impact on a generation of Presbyterian ministers trained in Glasgow, but he would also become a key figure in the Scottish Enlightenment, which emphasised human reason and conscience as the judge of all things.

Rev. Gilbert Kennedy

Rev. James Kirkpatrick was succeeded in 1743 by Rev. Gilbert Kennedy who was born in 1706, the son of Rev. Gilbert Kennedy of Tullylish. He was ordained at Lisburn by the Presbytery of Bangor on 7 June 1732 and installed as minister of Killyleagh Presbyterian Church, where he remained for over a decade until called by Second congregation. He was a member of the Synod of Ulster, rather than the Non-Subscribing Presbytery of Antrim and during his thirty years as minister Second congregation remained with the Synod of Ulster, where he was the moderator in 1763. During that year he made his view clear that it is *"unbecoming to be dogmatic in disputable matters"*. He was a strong supporter of religious freedom,

> *What is life without liberty? ... Love of liberty is a principle implanted and as deeply rooted in human nature as the love of life ... Truth will never flourish in the world till every degree of spiritual tyranny and domination over conscience be set aside, and men, delivered from the shackles and fetters of authority, be permitted without running any hazard freely to use their own reason and understanding in religious matters ... For what influence can that faith be supposed to have which stands only in the wisdom of men, and is not the result of impartial inquiry and rational conviction.*

Kennedy was the minister of Second congregation until 1773, the year he died on 12 May. The sermon at his funeral was preached by the then minister of First Belfast, Rev. James McKay. Kennedy is buried in Clifton Street Graveyard, Belfast. He was succeeded in 1773 by Rev. James Bryson (see profile), a member of the Synod of Ulster. Bryson was born in Holywood, County Down and was educated by notable Irish scholars. In 1762 he was licensed to preach by Armagh Presbytery and in the

20

following year was ordained a Presbyterian minister, subscribing in a less than fulsome manner to the Westminster Confession of Faith. He was minister of First Lisburn from 1763 to 1774 before being called to Second congregation in Rosemary Street Belfast where he stayed for nineteen years from 1773 to 1791. He often used a catch phrase, *"All the children of God are our brethren"*.

Despite the efforts of those who tried to insist on Subscription to the Westminster Confession of Faith, in 1783 ten out of the fourteen Presbyteries did not require subscription.

Members of Second congregation played a vitally important part in the development of the economy of Belfast, which expanded rapidly. Members opened the first bank in Belfast in 1751. In 1777 Robert Joy formed a partnership to build Belfast's first cotton mill in Francis Street. And with the success of this venture, Belfast was to become the centre of cotton production in Ireland. The Joy family (including Henry Joy, Henry Joy McCracken's uncle) owned Cromac Paper Mill and the *Belfast Newsletter* founded by Henry and Robert's grandfather, Francis. In 1783 Waddell Cunningham of Second congregation was a founder member and first chair of the Belfast Chamber of Commerce and two years later helped found and run the Harbour Corporation. In 1791 another member, William Ritchie, who had come from Saltcoats shipyard in Scotland, built a small boat repair yard on the banks of Lagan and the following year launched its first ship, *Hibernia*. The business expanded and was soon joined by a second yard established by his brother. This development eventually led to Belfast becoming the world leader in shipbuilding.

Rev. James Bryson

Some well known individuals associated with Second congregation

Rev. James Bryson*
(1730–1796)

James Bryson was born in 1730 in Holywood, County Down and was educated by notable Irish scholars the Lynches of Loughinisland. In 1762 he was licensed to preach by Armagh Presbytery and then ordained a minister in 1764, subscribing in an ambiguous manner to the Westminster Confession of Faith. He then became minister of First Lisburn in the same year. He was known as a liberal. He was called to Second congregation in 1773 where he stayed for nineteen years.

He was a keen supporter of the Belfast Society for the Promotion of Knowledge (now the Linenhall Library) and catalogued their books, along with the curator of the Society's museum, John Templeton. When the Volunteers were formed as a home guard against invasion by France, Rev. Bryson became the chairman and chaplain of Belfast First Volunteer Company. Following a dispute with Second congregation he founded the Fourth Presbyterian congregation in Belfast, in Donegall Street in 1792, where he served as minister until he died in 1797.

He had two sons, Samuel and Andrew who were also Irish speakers. Samuel was a military surgeon and later opened his own apothecary shop in Belfast. He was a key individual in the revival of the Irish language and one of the subscribers to Rev. William Neilson's *Introduction to the Irish language*, O'Reilly's *Irish Dictionary*, the Belfast Charitable Society and Belfast Harp Society. He is most notable as an Irish scholar and collector of Irish manuscripts. He wrote *Remains of the Irish Bards*. He died in 1863. His second son Andrew graduated from Glasgow University and was licensed by Bangor Presbytery. He was ordained in 1786 when he became the minister of Ballymascanlon Presbyterian Church, Dundalk from 1786 to 1795, where he frequently preached in Irish. He was asked to translate for the harpers at the Belfast Harp Society in 1791, but was unable to do so due to illness. He died in 1795.

---

* Sources: Bryson 1801 (ed Durey); Newman 1993; O Snodaigh 1995; Blaney 1996.

In 1773 the American War of Independence started. It was supported by large numbers of Irish Presbyterians who had emigrated. Its success by 1783 greatly encouraged political reformers in Ireland.

When the Volunteers were formed in 1778, as a home guard against invasion by France, James Bryson became the chairman and chaplain of Belfast First Volunteer Company. The Volunteer Companies were to play an important role in pressing for political reform. Bryson presided over a meeting of the Belfast Reading Society (which became the Belfast Library and Society for Promoting Knowledge and later the Linenhall Library), which declared its support for admitting Catholics to full and immediate participation enjoyed by their fellow citizens and countrymen. A committee set up by the volunteers, including Rev. Bryson made their view clear that,

> *More equal representation of the people in*
> *Parliament deserves the deliberate attention*
> *of every Irishman; as that alone which can*
> *perpetuate to future ages the inestimable*
> *possession of a free constitution.*

There was some reform through the Catholic Relief Act of 1778 and two years later the Test Act, which kept Presbyterians out of public office, was repealed. In 1782 Presbyterian ministers were given the right to officiate at marriages. For the Presbyterian radicals, however, this was all too little too late. Presbyterians could swear an oath, but still could not sit on juries, or give evidence in court in criminal cases. They could not be employed in positions of trust under the Crown.

In 1789 the French Revolution inspired many Presbyterians, including many in the Volunteer companies, to believe that real fundamental political change was

24

possible. Henry Joy, a moderate reformer and owner of the Belfast Newsletter, described its impact,

> *Encouraged by the success of these glorious efforts of the French nation, the friends of liberty in this country once more turned their undivided attention to the salutary measure of reform and renewed those efforts from which they had so ingloriously compelled to desist.*

Henry Joy went on to write a book entitled *Belfast Politics*. On 14 October 1791 The Society of United Irishmen was founded in secret by a group of Belfast Presbyterians, committed to radical political change. Tradition has it that the Belfast Society of United Irishmen met in a secret room above Second Church in Rosemary Street to avoid detection by the militia or government informers. Henry Joy found the plans of the United Irishmen too radical and did not support the rising.

Leading up to the rebellion Rev. William Sinclair, minister of Old Newtownards Presbyterian Church, and a founding member of the United Irishmen, spoke at a meeting in the Second Presbyterian Church in Belfast in December 1792. The meeting had been called to discuss *"the present state of public affairs, and to enter into such measure as might be deemed expedient for the accomplishment of the great object – an equal representation of the people in Parliament"*. He was eventually arrested for his part in the rising, but like many others was allowed to emigrate to America. In 1796 the Government passed the Insurrection Act to give them the power to crush the reform movement. Hundreds of northern Presbyterians were arrested. Many were flogged and their homes ransacked.

In 1797 Presbyterians in Ulster were enraged when William Orr was hung for administering a United Irish oath to two soldiers.

Some well known individuals associated with Second congregation

Robert Tennent*
(1765–1837)

Robert Tennent was born in Roseyards, near Ballymena, Co. Antrim on 9 August 1765, the son of Seceder minister Rev John Tennant, who was one of the original subscribers to the radical newspaper, *Northern Star*. Robert became a doctor and was a member of Second congregation, unlike his brother William, who was a member of First Church and a founding member of the United Irishmen. He was working as a ship's surgeon when the Table Bay mutiny took place and was out of the country during the 1798 rebellion.

Dr Robert Tennent was one of the founders of the Belfast Academical Institution. He chaired a St Patrick's day dinner of the joint Boards of the Institution at which, allegedly, disloyal toasts were drunk by the founders (many of whom had been United Irishmen), which resulted in serious problems for the school from its conservative detractors in Government and Synod, including the loss of the annual government grant of £1,500. At the dinner he called for the establishment of a new society, a

> *"centre of union to those who love their country" to promote the "eternal principle of equal, impartial justice". He argued that, "were this standard once erected in our land and the people but convinced that it were so – how soon would all our lamentable dissensions vanish and the Irish character be again displayed in all its native beauty and excellence."*

In 1813 he organised a public meeting to discuss the nature of Orangeism, which had played such a negative role in promoting sectarianism and preventing democratic reforms. Rev. Edward May, an Episcopal minister and son-in-law of the Marquis of Donegal, who owned most of the land in Belfast, attempted to prevent the meeting and Dr. Tennent and Rev. May came to blows. Tennent was arrested and imprisoned. He later sued, unsuccessfully, for unlawful imprisonment.

---

* Sources: McBride 1998; Newman 1993; Brooke 1994; Holmes 1985; Campbell 1991.

After 1813, the supporters of Catholic Emancipation, led by Robert Tennent and William Drennan of the Friends of Civil and Religious Liberty managed to secure significant support in the House of Commons.

Tennent was to play a key role in most of the progressive developments in Belfast, including the establishment of the Fever Hospital and the Belfast House of Industry to provide work for the poor. The Society closed with the passing of the Poor Law Act.

He also played an important role in providing clean water to the citizens of Belfast as a member of the Pipe Water Committee of the Belfast Charitable Society and was a Spring Water Commissioner from 1817. In 1828 he was appointed President of the Belfast Society for the Promotion of Knowledge (now the Linenhall Library) and served until he died in 1837.

His son, Robert James, stood for parliament with William Sharman Crawford, but failed to win a seat because he refused to declare his views on a repeal of the Act of Union. He was also on the board of the Belfast Academical Institution.

His third son, John Tennent Jr, born in 1772 became involved in the United Irishmen, fled to France and died in the service of Napoleon, aged 41.

Presbyterian meeting houses were often focal points for the public expression of the dissatisfaction of the dissenting community at their treatment at the hands of the Ascendancy. For example, in December 1792 a general meeting of the inhabitants of Belfast (which by this stage had risen to 18,000) was held in the Second congregation meetinghouse,

> *For the purpose of expressing their sentiments on the present state of public affairs, and to enter into such measures as may be deemed expedient for the accomplishing that great object, an equal representation of the People in parliament.*

In 1798 the United Irishmen, who in Ulster where made up primarily of Presbyterians, led a rising against authoritarian and oppressive rule, under which Presbyterians and Catholics experienced terrible discrimination and economic injustice. With the plans of the rising having been passed on to the authorities by spies, many of the leaders had already been arrested and the rising was quickly put down by the authorities. Many of the leaders who participated were executed or allowed to emigrate to America.

Although it has been suggested that those Presbyterians who participated in the rising were mainly "New Light" theologically, in *Scripture Politics*, McBride has shown that the fifty Presbyterian ministers and licentiates who actively participated in the rising were fairly equally divided between new and old light supporters. The only Presbyterian minister in Belfast who was officially implicated in the rising was Sinclair Kelburn of Third Belfast who was "Old Light" Calvinist theologically. After the French Revolution when France and Britain were at war, the Revs. Patrick Vance, and James Bryson were stung by accusations that they had prayed for military victory by the French over the British and wrote saying the accusation was groundless. To prove the point, or to deflect suspicion,

28

the day after the Battle of Antrim in 1798, Vance joined
Rev. William Bruce as a volunteer in the Yeomen guard,
which helped put down the rebellion. He died on 2 January
1800.

Rev. Bryson accepted a call to a new Belfast congregation,
later to become Cliftonville Church in North Belfast in
1792, where he was minister until he died in 1796. With
Rev. James Bryson's move on 1 August 1791, Rev. Patrick
Vance was installed as minister of Second congregation.
He had been born in 1756, the son of the Rev. Thomas
Vance of Ushers Quay Dublin, who died in 1772. He was
licensed by the Synod of Munster and ordained in
Sommerhill, County Meath on 2 May 1779. He remained in
Second congregation for nine years until he died in 1800.
Under Rev. Vance Second congregation returned to the
Non-Subscribing Presbytery of Antrim. Vance and three
other members of Second congregation were subscribers to
the establishment of the Old Poorhouse in Clifton Street
Belfast, which became the Belfast Charitable Society.

With concern about the legal ownership of the original
meetinghouse in Rosemary Street, the site in Rosemary
Lane was formally leased from the Earl of Donegall.
In 1789, Second Church was demolished and a new larger
Church built.

Following the suppression of the 1798 Rebellion the
Government enacted the Act of Union in 1801, which did
away with the unpopular and oppressive Irish Government
in Dublin, which had been controlled by the minority
Episcopal authorities. In the early part of the century many
of those involved in the rising emigrated to America, either
voluntarily, to avoid arrest, or as part of their sentence.
Some of those remaining turned their minds to other kinds
of reform such as education, or to cultural activities, and
later in the century, to the rights of tenant farmers.

Some well known individuals associated with the Second congregation

Samuel Martin Stephenson*
(1742–1733)

Samuel Stephenson was born in Straidballymorris, County Antrim in 1742, the youngest son of James Stephenson. He was educated in Glasgow University and in 1773 was licensed by Templepatrick Presbytery. He was a non-subscriber and was ordained in Greyabbey and became their minister. However, some members of Bangor Presbytery refused to attend his ordination because he would not subscribe to the Westminster Confession of Faith and created the Presbytery of Belfast in protest. The following year he published his *"Declaration of faith approved of by the Reverend Presbytery of Bangor"*, which produced a pamphlet in response from the Rev. John King.

Whilst a minister he studied medicine and graduated as a doctor. Although there were various ministers who also practiced as doctors, Stephenson chose to resign as a minister in 1785 and concentrate on his medical practice and became a leading medical practitioner in Belfast, revitalising the treatment of fever cases. He was succeeded at Greyabbey by Rev. James Porter who, after the 1798 rising, was arrested and hung.

Stephenson regularly carried out scientific experiments and was one of the founders of the Belfast Dispensary in 1792 and of the Fever Hospital in 1797. In 1793 he joined the Belfast Society for the promotion of Knowledge and regularly attended meetings. In 1808 he produced a publication on the *Linen and Hempen Manufactures in the Province of Ulster*. He was elected president of the Belfast Society in 1817. He was a vigorous supporter of the Belfast Academical Institution, which opened in 1814. He was held in such high regard that the Church decided to honour him by replacing his name on the list of active ministers.

He resigned his practice in favour of his son, Robert in 1821 and applied himself to farming and church history, producing publications on the parishes and congregations of both Greyabbey and Templepatrick. He died on 13 January 1833, aged 91.

---

* Sources: Killen 1990, Montgomery 1925.

Rev. Vance died in 1800 and was succeeded as minister of Second congregation by newly ordained Rev. William Hamilton Drummond (see profile), aged 22. Drummond remained minister for fifteen years up to 1815, by which time there were 450 members of the congregation.

In 1806 Second Belfast was the first Presbyterian congregation to install an organ in the church, which was, at that time, a very controversial move, as many in the Presbyterian Church opposed the use of any form of instrument in worship, preferring precentors who led the singing instead. Tradition has it that the organ installed in Second Church by Edward Bunting (see profile) had previously been installed in St George's Chapel Windsor, England and had been played by George Frederick Handel in front of the King. Bunting informed the congregation of the availability of the organ in 1801 and the congregation purchased it in 1806, dedicating it to the *"Glory of the Almighty"* at a service led by Rev. Drummond, which included Lord Castlereagh. Edward Bunting had previously been organist at St Anne's Cathedral, but had been refused permission to organise cultural events there, so moved to Second congregation and remained there until 1817. He was to organise the first ever Belfast Musical Festival in Second Church, with a choir and orchestra from Dublin performing the Messiah.

With a gift from John Montgomery, chair of the Church Committee, as a memorial to his daughter, Agnes, who died in June 1901, the organ was eventually replaced with a new one in 1928. The old organ was sold to First Newry Non-Subscribing congregation who employed an architect, Edmund Barre to remove it from Second Church, transport it and install it in the church in Newry, where it was dedicated on the 28 November 1928.

Rev. William Hamilton Drummond

Rev. William Hamilton Drummond*
(1778–1865)

William Drummond was born in Larne, County Antrim in 1778, son of Dr. William Drummond, a naval surgeon, and Rose (nee Hare). He was educated at Belfast Academy and Glasgow University. Poverty prevented him completing his studies. He discovered, however, a great gift for writing poetry and prose and wrote various publications, including *The Man of Age*, which describes the poverty of the peasants in Ireland at that time. Drummond asserted that Ireland was *"labouring under desperate mismanagement"* and although there is no evidence that he took part in the 1798 rebellion, he was in Larne when the rebellion was taking place and was stopped by a group of loyalists returning from battle, bent on revenge for the death of Lord O'Neill. They put a pistol to his head saying *"you young villain, it is you and the like of you brought this upon us, with your infernal poetry!"* Fortunately he was saved by his companion who averted the soldier's gun.

He was licensed by the Antrim Presbytery in 1800, without having to subscribe to the Westminster Confession of Faith and became the minister of Second congregation, where he installed the first organ in a Presbyterian Church in Ireland and composed a number of hymns himself. He was a founder and active member of the Belfast Literary Society and, as well as running a school in his own house, Mount Collyer, was a strong supporter of the Belfast Academical Institution. In 1810 a Doctorate of Divinity was conferred on him by Aberdeen University. In 1815 he received a call from Strand Street church in Dublin, to work with Rev. Dr. James Armstrong, which gave him more time for his writing.

He was a strong believer of the place of reason in religion and was opposed to the concepts of the Trinity and original sin. In 1827, he published *"The Doctrine of the Trinity, founded neither on Scripture, nor on Reason and Common Sense, but on Tradition and the Infallible Church*. In 1840 he published an edited autobiography of the radical United Irishman, Archibald Hamilton Rowan. He died in Dublin in 1865.

---

* Sources: Haire 1981; Blaney 1996; Hill et al 1998.

On 10 March 1810 Samuel Ferguson was born in High Street Belfast and was baptised by Rev. Drummond in Second Church, where Rev. Vance had married his parents in 1799. Sir Samuel Ferguson would go on to become one of the most famous poets and antiquarians to come out of Ulster.

Rev. William Dalzell Huey McEwen (see profile) became the minister of Second congregation in 1817, after having been minister of First Killyleagh. He died young in 1828, while still the minister of Second congregation.

In the early part of the nineteenth century, the members of the Second Presbyterian congregation in Belfast, along with many former United Irishmen, were strong supporters of the establishment of an Academical Institution which could be both a non-sectarian inter-denominational school and a training college for students for the ministry. The Second congregation supported it financially when it was established in 1810 and provided seats in the gallery for students from the Institution. In 1817 the church raised a fund to pay for the appointment of a Professor of Divinity at the Institution.

In 1821 Belfast established the first fever hospital in Ireland, designed for one hundred patients, which was immediately overwhelmed with fever patients. In 1837 there were at one time 251 fever patients in the hospital, with up to three to a bed. An Annex had to be obtained from the Belfast Academical Institution to hold a further one hundred patients. At one stage it housed over four hundred patients. The House Surgeon and Assistant House Surgeon died from contracting typhus from the patients. In the 1830s smallpox was also of serious concern. An epidemic of typhus followed hard on the heels of the famine with over five thousand being admitted between April 1847 and March 1848, 13.4% of whom died.

Some well known individuals associated with the Second congregation

Edward Bunting*
(1773–1843)
Edward Bunting was born in Armagh in 1773. He was very talented musically and was sent to study music in Drogheda. At the age of eleven he was appointed sub-organist, to William Ware at St Anne's Cathedral in Belfast. While in Belfast he stayed with the politically progressive Presbyterian McCracken family and became close friends with Henry Joy McCracken. He earned his living by teaching music.

He became interested in traditional Irish music and became concerned that much of the tradition was going to be lost within a few years. When the famous Belfast Harp Festival was organised in 1792, to coincide with the commemoration of the storming of the Bastille, bringing together ten harpists from all over Ireland and even one from Wales, Bunting was employed to transcribe the tunes played by the harpists, sparking a lifelong involvement in collecting ancient Irish tunes. Following the Belfast Harp Festival, Bunting went on a series of tours to Derry, Tyrone and Connaught to find and transcribe the tunes of traditional musicians. In 1796 he published "*A General Collection of the Ancient Irish Music*".

In St Anne's Cathedral, Bunting was keen to organise musical evenings and events, but was refused permission. As a result he left the Cathedral to become organist of Second congregation in 1806, overseeing the installation of the first organ in a Presbyterian Church in Ireland. Bunting remained the organist of Second congregation for eleven years.

In 1813 Bunting organised the first Belfast Musical Festival in Second Church featuring the first almost complete performance of Handel's Messiah. In 1819 Bunting married and decided to move to Dublin where he became the organist of St George's Church. His final collection of harp airs, "The Ancient Music of Ireland" was published in 1840. He died on 21 December 1843 and is buried in Mount Jerome Cemetery.

---

* Sources: Newman 1993; Bradbury 2002.

In 1854 cholera returned to Belfast. In 1851/2 Rev. John Porter and seventeen other clergymen of various denominations signed a letter of appeal to the public for their support of the hospital.

Second congregation always had a strong pioneering medical tradition of doctors with a wide concern for society, as well as their patients. These medical practitioners included Samuel Martin Stephenson 1742–1833 who was vice-president and president of the Belfast Reading Society for twenty-five years and founding member of the Belfast Academical Institution (see profile); Andrew Malcolm 1818–1857 (see profile); Sir John Campbell, who opened the Rosemary Hall, and officiated at many Second congregation functions, as well as writing a *History of the Non-Subscribing Presbyterian Church in Ireland*; Hugh G Callwell, who wrote a biography of Dr Malcolm and whose sister married Rev. Agnew; right through to Mollie McGeown 1923–2004 (see profile).

Second congregation provided an annual allowance for Rev William Steele Dickson, who, as a key figure in the United Irishmen, had so eloquently articulated the theological case for the need for political reform, which has been described as "Scripture Politics". After his arrest and imprisonment for his part in the 1798 rising he was no longer made welcome by all those who had sought his counsel and company before the failed rising. Without patronage he suffered great poverty and was given a weekly allowance by the Second congregation. When he died he was buried in a pauper's grave, at a ceremony officiated at by Rev. W. D. H. McEwen, the minister of Second congregation, and attended by only nine or ten people.

Rev. W D H McEwen

Some well known individuals associated with the Second congregation

Rev. William Dalzell Huey McEwen*
(1787–1828)

McEwen was born in 1787, the eldest son of Rev. George McEwen, the Presbyterian minister of Killinchy. He was educated in Glasgow University, receiving his MA in 1806 and was licensed to preach by the Belfast Presbytery in 1807, subscribing to the Westminster Confession of Faith. He was ordained in 1808 in Usher's Quay, Dublin, as a colleague of Rev. Hugh Moore. He married Jane Maxwell, whose father Thomas Maxwell came from Ballygraffan near Comber and was implicated in the 1798 rising, arrested and put to death.

McEwen was installed in 1813 by the Presbytery of Dromore in First Killyleagh congregation, County Down, of which the radical Archibald Rowan Hamilton was a member. McEwen was initially believed to be evangelical in theology but became "New Light". In 1825, whilst minister of Second congregation, he invited John Smithurst, an English Socinian, who disputed the divinity of Jesus, to preach. When McEwen was called to Second congregation in 1817, he was succeeded in Killyleagh by Henry Cooke, who would later become the leading arch-Conservative in the Presbyterian Church in Ireland. McEwen remained at Second congregation until his death.

Along with his ministerial duties, he became a part-time Professor of Elocution at the Belfast Academical Institution and was accused, along with two others, of holding unorthodox theological views by Henry Cooke. While a lecturer there he gave volumes of the works of Unitarian, Dr Richard Price, as prizes to his pupils, which enraged the strictly orthodox Cooke. He was later secretary of the Institution and spent much time in London lobbying MPs to have the Institution's annual grant restored, which was achieved in 1828.

He acted as temporary editor of the *Northern Whig* for a while. He died in College Square Belfast in 1828, at the relatively young age of 41 and was buried in Killinchy. He left his wife, Jane and six children.

---

* Sources: Brooke 1994; McCreery 1875; Notes provided by Rev John Nelson.

Some of those who opposed subscription to the Westminster Confession of Faith did so on the grounds that the Bible and human conscience should be the only standard of faith, others were Arian in belief and did not accept the doctrine of the Trinity, which had been drawn up at the Council of Nicea (325 AD) For a considerable amount of time in Britain and Ireland it was actually against the law to criticise the doctrine of the Trinity. However, in 1817 it eventually stopped being illegal to impugn the doctrine of the Holy Trinity, so it became easier for Unitarians to publicly express their views.

In 1828, the peaceful co-existence between the supporters and opponents of subscription to the Westminster Confession of Faith, with the establishment of the Non-Subscribing Presbytery of Antrim, erupted when Synod decided to introduce a compulsory test of the orthodoxy of all students for the ministry. This further exacerbated the long-running dispute between arch-conservative Rev. Henry Cooke and non-subscriber Rev. Henry Montgomery, each with their respective supporters. Eventually, in 1830, a group of seventeen Non-Subscribing ministers and congregations, led by Montgomery created the Remonstrant Synod made up of the three Presbyteries of Armagh, Bangor and Templepatrick and left the fellowship of The Presbyterian Church in Ireland.

Many other Presbyterian ministers who supported non-subscription decided to remain within the main Synod of Ulster. Rev. Henry Cooke, however, was not prepared to leave it at that and tried to prevent the Non-Subscribing congregations from retaining their church buildings and property. His tactics included sending young probationers to harass older Non-Subscribing ministers during and after Sunday services. When Cooke tried to take over the meetinghouse of Rev. William Glendy of Ballycarry, the congregation got wind of his plans and a thousand people were ready for him when he arrived and prevented him entering the church and holding a meeting in the Main Street. The crowd burnt an effigy of Cooke. Cooke also asked landowner William Montgomery to evict Rev. John Watson from his church in Greyabbey. As a result, Watson was arrested, and detained for 8 or 9 hours. He was eventually released and reinstated in Greyabbey. Second congregation, which was already a member of the Non-Subscribing Synod of Antrim did not face any challenges over its property.

The exit of the Non-Subscribing ministers and congregations from the Synod of Ulster left the way clear for a rapprochement between the Synod of Ulster and Calvinist Seceders, who eventually formally joined together as the Presbyterian Church in Ireland in 1840.

At this point the population of Belfast had increased to over 50,000 and would double within twenty years. The Catholic population, in particular, had continued to increase and two new chapels were opened that year. Two years later St Malachy's School was opened.

Following the early death of Rev. McEwen, in May 1829, Rev. John Porter, from County Tyrone, who was born in 1800 and educated at Belfast Academical Institution, preached on trial in Second Church, after two years in Toxteth Park Liverpool. The following month the congregation agreed to call him as their minister. He was ordained by the Presbytery of Antrim on 6 August 1829 and became their minister. At the meeting after his ordination, chaired by John S Ferguson, amongst others who spoke, was Right Rev. William Crolly, Bishop of Down & Connor, who became the Catholic Archbishop of Armagh and Lord Primate of Ireland. The address was given by Rev Bruce.

Some well known individuals associated with the Second congregation

Robert Shipboy MacAdam*
(1808–1895)

Robert MacAdam was born in Belfast in 1808, the son of James MacAdam a hardware merchant, and Jane (nee Shipboy). He was educated at the recently opened Belfast Academical Institution from 1818, when he was 10 years old. He became a member of the Non-Subscribing Second Presbyterian Church in Rosemary Street Belfast. After he left school he was apprenticed to his father's hardware business. However, when he was only 13 his father died.

In the same year, despite his young age, he was present when the Belfast Natural History and Philosophical Society was formed in 1821. While making visits around Ireland for his father's firm, he developed a fluency in the Irish language, which he was probably taught by William Neilson while at the Belfast Academical Institutio. In 1835 he wrote an *"Irish grammar"* for use in language classes at the Belfast Academical Institution and was involved in the establishment of various Irish language Schools. He began to collect folk tales in Irish while on his travels. He also collected Gaelic manuscripts, including many ancient Irish texts and personally translated many texts from Irish. He was a founding member and co-secretary of the Ulster Gaelic Society, established in 1828.

He began a retail business in Townsend Street Belfast, with his brother James, in 1838, which they sold two years later, along with their house, in order to raise the capital in order to start the Soho foundry in Townsend Street, producing a wide range of iron products.

In the early 1850s he was a leading organiser and promoter of an exhibition of Irish antiquities in the Belfast Museum, which led to the formation of the *Ulster Journal of Archaeology*, of which he was the editor for the first eleven years. The journal made a crucial contribution to the preservation and promotion of Irish antiquities, culture and language. He was also a member of the Linenhall Library and the Harmonic and Harp Societies.

He died in 1895 leaving a lasting legacy, including a large number of ancient manuscripts in the Irish language which he had collected.

---

* Sources: Blaney 1996; Newman 1993; Bradbury 2002.

41

Under Rev. Porter's leadership, in the first year of his ministry the Second congregation established a Circulating Theological Library and the following year started a course of evening lectures in the church, with cheap rates for the working classes. Up to this point the church had no form of lighting, so evening activities were restricted to the summer months, or to the exceptional use of candles. By the end of the decade, however, gas lighting had been fitted in the church.

In 1825 a Parliamentary Commission of Enquiry into Irish Education led, in 1831, to a proposal to introduce a national system of education throughout Ireland. The initial proposals were for a non-sectarian system of integrated education, which were opposed by powerful church forces. The revised proposals created denominational schools and allowed the existing books to be replaced by books prepared by the denominations. The General Meeting of the Association of Non-Subscribing Presbyterian Churches criticized the revised proposals, which reversed the original official policy of non-denominational education, saying that they would denominationalise the whole country.

In 1839 Rev. Porter established a day and Sunday school in Castle Street, Belfast, with forty day scholars, run by a Miss Anderson. Three years later it had expanded to 84 pupils, and had become part of the Irish National Education system, requiring a move to larger premises in Fountain Street known as the Gymnasium, teaching reading, writing, grammar, arithmetic, geography and natural philosophy.

The Remonstrant Synod of Ulster joined with the Presbytery of Antrim, which Second congregation was already a member of, in 1835 to form the Association of Irish Non-Subscribing Presbyterians. By 1838 the congregation had a membership of around 200 families, containing over a thousand individuals. By 1840 the Sunday School had 275 children and 28 teachers.

Rev. John Porter

The Dissenters Chapels Act of 1844 finally resolved the various disputes over ownership of church buildings following the creation of the Remonstrant Synod of Ulster. It allowed the Non-Subscribing congregations, which had joined the Remonstrant Synod to retain their church buildings and other property.

The grievances that so many Presbyterians had fought for in 1798 were gradually addressed during the nineteenth century. The Reform Act of 1832 finally gave Presbyterians the right to stand for Parliament on their own terms without landlord nomination.

A major grievance of Presbyterians over the previous hundred years was the lack of recognition of Presbyterian marriages, with implications for recognition of children and legacies. In 1842 the Second congregation petitioned Parliament in support of amendments to the Marriage Laws, which would finally end discrimination against Presbyterian marriages. The same year this was finally fully corrected by legislation, which gave Presbyterian marriages the same status as marriages solemnised in the Established Church.

In December 1845 Frederick Douglass, a former escaped slave and famous anti-slavery campaigner, gave a lecture in the Second congregation church hall on behalf of the Anti-Slavery Society. He toured Britain and Ireland to avoid being recaptured by his "owner" and published his autobiography, *Narrative of the Life of Frederick Douglass, an American Slave*. Douglass' visit to Second congregation was particularly ironic as it was a member of Second congregation, Waddell Cunningham, reputed to be the wealthiest man in Belfast at the time, with a plantation in the West Indies, who had proposed that Ireland should get involved in the lucrative slave trade. It is supposed to be Thomas McCabe, a watch-maker, who became a leading

United Irishman, who put a stop to the proposal by writing in Cunningham's subscription book, *"May God eternally damn the soul of the man who subscribes the first guinea"*. As a result Wolf Tone used to refer to Thomas McCabe as "The Irish Slave". S Shannon Millin (see profile), the historian of Second congregation, argued that Waddell Cunningham was wrongly identified as the promoter of slavery in this story, but was forced to back down when presented with the overwhelming evidence.

In 1849 Queens College in South Belfast, with its magnificent Lanyon building, was finally completed and lectures began in November.

By 1851, despite a series of typhus, cholera and influenza epidemics, the population of Belfast had almost doubled over the previous twenty years, averaging two families per house. By 1858 the Second congregation had 751 members in 177 families, substantially larger than that of First Belfast.

Second congregation, during this period, was not only concerned with spiritual affairs. With continued discrimination against dissenters in appointments to certain positions in education and elsewhere, in 1852 the congregation petitioned both Houses of Parliament in support of abolition of any sectarian tests in the appointment of professorships of secular learning and other non-religious posts.

In April 1868 the Second congregation sent another petition, which was signed by Rev. Porter, as well as the chairman and secretary of the congregation, to the House of Commons in support of the Disestablishment of the Church of Ireland,

Some well known individuals associated with the Second congregation

Dr. Andrew George Malcolm*
1818–1857

Andrew Malcolm was born in Newry in 1818, the sixth child of Rev. Andrew George Malcom, a Non-Subscribing minister in Newry, and Eleanor (nee Hunter). Unfortunately his father died of typhus fever in 1823.

In 1829, the family moved to York Street, Belfast and became members of Second congregation. Malcolm was educated at Belfast Academical Institution. So highly regarded was he as a student, that the Professor, Rev. Henry Montgomery, appointed him as an assistant. He then moved to Edinburgh to study medicine and qualified in 1842. He worked as a student in Frederick Street Fever Hospital in Belfast and wrote his thesis on *Pathology and continuing fever*. He then started a medical practice from his mother's house in York Street and was appointed as voluntary District Medical Attendant with the charity Belfast General Dispensary, to the poor in North Belfast, where he was involved in visiting working class homes, as well as working out of the hospital. When the Dispensary was re-organised on a more professional basis, he was then givn a paid position.

He was appointed as an attending physician at the Fever Hospital in 1845. From his experience with families in the area, he was concerned about the "*slave-labour of the working people*" and the health of the large number of workers, from as young as ten, employed in the unregulated textile mills. He wrote a paper in 1855 on "*The influence of factory life on the health of operatives*". Malcolm strongly supported the Ten Hour Act, which limited the number of daily hours worked each day. He encouraged employers to facilitate the education of their workforce and to establish reading clubs and music societies for their employees.

Malcolm founded the Belfast Working Classes Association for the promotion of general improvement. It developed a popular reading room and in 1847 published its own campaigning magazine, *The Belfast People's Magazine*, to try to bring about improvement in housing and sanitation, as well as moral and

---

* Sources: Newman 1993; Bardon 1992; Calwell 1973 & 1977.

recreational improvements. He was clear that the "*education of the working classes has been for a long time too much neglected*". The Association opened a circulating library to make books and newspapers available to those who couldn't otherwise afford them. He organised lectures on topics like *Education for Women, Sanitation,* and *Adulteration of Food, The Social Position of the Working Classes* and *Practical Education.*

In 1845 he decided that the priority was the provision of public baths and washing houses, because of the lack of such facilities in the homes of the poor. He visited similar facilities in English towns and was eventually successful in building a public baths and washing house in Belfast. Unfortunately it ran into financial trouble and despite campaigning for it to be taken over by the town council, it closed. He was also an active member of the Belfast Social Enquiry Society which campaigned for the opening of a public park.

When the Great Irish famine hit in 1845, there was an outbreak of fever and a Board of Health was established in Belfast and Malcolm became one of the officers of the Board to try and tackle the outbreak, although with such poor sanitation and housing there was only a limited amount they could do. A year later, as the epidemic subsided, the Board of Health was abolished despite objections from Malcolm, who called for a permanent health body.
In 1847 he published the findings of sanitary inspections he conducted in north Belfast. He was deeply concerned about the level of overcrowding, poor ventilation, almost non-existent sanitary provision, the lack of clean water and the impact of these conditions on the health of families and the ever-present danger of disease. He dramatically said, "*the churchyards have been fattened with the children of toil, and the poor-houses are thronged with their orphans*". Despite facing apathy he continued with his lobbying for improvements to drainage, ventilation, water to every house, street cleaning, public lavatories and strict control of the building of new houses. In response the town council eventually established the Belfast Sanitary Committee. With the ending of the cholera epidemic of 1848, however, the town council decided to close it down.

Malcolm published a *History of the General Hospital and other Medical Institutions in Belfast,* in 1851, which he hoped would generate support for the hospital. He died of heart disease on 19 September 1856. A member of the Second congregation, Dr. Hugh G. Calwell, wrote his biography.

*Petitioners are of the opinion that wherever great
diversities of faith exist in a nation the establishment
of any particular sect is most impolitic. But in
Ireland, where an insignificant minority is thus
honoured and elevated, such an institution becomes
utterly indefencible. Jealousies, heart-burnings,
hatreds are the inevitable consequences. To this
more than any cause do petitioners ascribe the
strong and general dislike to British rule which,
since the origin of the Established Church in
Ireland, would appear to be deepening and
spreading from generation to generation up to
the present day.*

In 1870 the Government finally ended the Episcopal
Church's dominant position as the Established Church in
Ireland. From that point all churches were considered to be
of equal standing. Along with this the regium donum state
grant to ministers came to an end. To include congregations
which had become independent of The Association of Non-
Subscribing Presbyterian Churches the name of the
Association was enlarged to become The Association of
Non-Subscribing Presbyterian and other Free Churches.
Having served the congregation for over forty years, in
1870, Rev. Porter asked the congregation to call a new
minister, and Rev. James C. Street (see profile), from
Newcastle-Upon-Tyne, was installed in 1871 as the minister
of the reopened newly renovated Second Church in
Rosemary Street and was welcomed at a very large *Soiree
and Conversazione* in Belfast attended by 1,400 members
of Second congregation, other congregations and special
guests. For the first three years he shared the ministry with
Rev. Porter, who died in 1874. Rev. Street remained the
minister of the Second congregation until 1890. Rev. Street,
according to Rev. James Kennedy of Larne, was keen to
"revolutionise our various institutions" and as a result
"our church became convulsed and worse".

Rev. James Christopher Street

Some well known individuals associated with the Second congregation

Rev. James Christopher Street*
(1832–1911)

James Street was born in Nottingham in 1832, son of Christopher Street. He was ordained in Manchester in 1860 and for the next three years was a Manchester Superintendent Missionary. In 1863 he became the minister of a non-conformist church in Newcastle-upon-Tyne. In 1871 he moved to the Second congregation. He was involved in controversy even before he took up his position, because of his pro-Congregationalist views, which meant that he believed he should be installed by the congregation, not by the Presbytery, made up of ministers. This eventually resulted in the congregation withdrawing from the Presbytery of Antrim and forming the Free Congregational Union.

Street was not only theologically progressive, but also committed to demonstrating his faith through practical action. Within months of his arrival in Belfast he set up a scheme for erecting schools alongside the Church, where both Sunday Schools and congregational meetings could be held. He also founded the Rosemary Street Mutual Improvement Association, which sought to improve the intellectual, social and moral advancement of its members, regardless of religious denomination. He was also involved in the development of the Royal Victoria Hospital and, for his efforts, was made a life governor. He was also involved in a range of other initiatives to help the poor in the city. He was also a strong supporter of tenant right and often spoke and preached on behalf of tenant farmers.

He published many pamphlets and sermons, including *What is Unitariansim?; Why Labour to Extend our Faith?; What is a Christian?; The Half-way House to Infidelity;* and *Communings with the Father: Collects and Prayers* (edited by his son, also a Unitarian minister).

In 1890 he returned to England and ended his career with positions in Northampton, Birmingham and Shrewsbury. He retired in 1908 and died in 1911. His son Christopher James Street also became a Unitarian minister.

---

* Sources: Campbell 1991; McMillen; Notes prepared by Rev. John Nelson.

Under Rev. Street's influence, on 24 October 1871, Second congregation withdrew from the Presbytery of Antrim and formed a Congregational Union, with Moneyrea, Mountpottinger and part of the Carrickfergus congregation. The Congregational Union applied to join the The Association of Non-Subscribing Presbyterian and other Free Churches, but was rejected, as were the individual members of the Union when they applied.

The year that Rev. Street was installed, the interior of Second church in Rosemary Street was refurbished. The old pews were replaced with more modern bench pews and the old pulpit was replaced with a platform pulpit. The original sounding board over the pulpit was turned into a beautiful round table and was moved into the vestry in the church.

Continuing Second Church's commitment to education, in 1872, the foundation stone for a school was laid next to the church. In November of the same year Rev. Street established the Rosemary Street Mutual Improvement Association, the earliest of its kind in Belfast, which sought to improve the intellectual, social and moral advancement of its members, regardless of their religious denomination.

The Rosemary Street Improvement Association had a reading room and weekly meetings for debate. These had a reputation for open discussion on any topic without restriction. Topics included *Buddha: His life and teachings; Prejudice; Count Tolstoi and Russian Society*. Rev. Street, as President of the Association, spoke on *Lights and Shadows of Life in Belfast* as well as about his extensive travels.

Rev. Street was involved in other initiatives to help the poor, including a Coal Fund and the Royal Hospital. During the very severe frost of 1879 he helped establish relief works along with Vere Foster (see profile).

Special Feature

Domestic Mission

Conscious of the level of poverty in Belfast and the number of people who had moved to the city to escape from the even more terrible rural poverty, in 1853, the First and Second congregations got together and established a Belfast Domestic Mission. Mr A McIntyre from Dublin was appointed to run it from premises on the corner of William Street and John Street off Divis Street. He was horrified by the extent of poverty that he found and recorded some of his experiences,

> *1 September 1853: Spent the forenoon of to-day in getting two poor children into the Union workhouse. I met these two little boys on the Queen's Bridge. The first thing that arrested my attention was the circumstance of the elder abusing the younger. He was dashing his head on the crib stones. A woman ... passing at the time stated that the elder was drowning the younger two days before but that some boys prevented him. I learnt ... that the father was killed by some accident a few years ago ..., that the mother and children had been in the workhouse some year or so ago but that she had come out and brought the children with her and that lately she has had to go to the hospital being ill of dropsy and that now the children have no-one to ... take care of them. They were both all but naked, and when I saw that the elder had to carry the younger on his back and beg whatever they got, I could not think it strange that he should sometimes be driven by hunger and fatigue to acts of cruelty and desperation.*

A day school was opened under John Burke and they soon had over 65 pupils and a Sunday school with 60 pupils and 15 volunteer teachers from the two congregations. Not long after, it came under the National Education Board. It also established evening classes for more advanced young people.

During this period Belfast was ravaged by an outbreak of cholera, affecting many of the families attending the mission, as witnessed by the women from the two congregations who made up the Ladies Visiting Committee.

Running the mission in a very impoverished part of Belfast was clearly not an easy task and the superintendents tended not to stay very long. In 1857/8 McIntyre resigned to be succeeded by Rev. Thomas Rutherford, who stayed until 1860. Rev. Henry Eachus was appointed, but only lasted a couple of years before taking up the ministry in Pudsey. He was succeeded by Rev. Thomas Bowring.

The Mission attracted a considerable number of children to the Girls and Boys clubs and families who were in receipt of hand-outs of tea, groceries, clothes and coal, especially at Christmas, and quickly outgrew the premises it had moved to at 90 Donegall Street. Valentine Whitla provided the land and paid for the construction of a new mission building in Stanhope Street, off Clifton Street, and then paid for a new school (which became Malvern Street School). He then provided the money for the furnishings for both premises, which opened in May 1864. Within three months of opening, however, sectarian rioting engulfed the area causing serious difficulties.

The move of Second congregation into a Congregational Union, under Rev. Street, created a conflict with the Domestic Mission and Rev. Street established another Domestic Mission in Hopeton Street Belfast, which did not prove to be particularly successful.

Sources:
The Non-Subscribing Presbyterian

By 1881 the population of Belfast was over 208,000, having multiplied more than fifteen times over the previous one hundred years. Seven years later Belfast was granted the official status as a city.

In January 1881 Rev. Street edited the *Chronicle and Index of the Unitarian Society Belfast*, highlighting their activities and publications. Several months later, in April, the church hosted the Jubilee meeting of the Unitarian Society.

Demonstrating that inter-faith activities are not a product of the last few years, in July 1883 Baboo Protap Chunder Mozoomdar preached in Second Church, including a Brahmo Somaj ritual and Hindu readings as well as texts from the Bible.

In 1887, the year of the Queen's Jubilee, the Association of Non-Subscribing Presbyterian and other Free Churches created the Orphan Society, to care for children whose parents had died. Thomas Henderson of Second congregation was the treasurer from 1907 to 1913.

In 1890 Rev. Street returned to England and the following year Rev. Edgar I. Fripp (see profile), another Englishman, who had been a minister in Mansfield, Nottinghamshire, was installed as minister of Second congregation. Even before he was formally installed he spoke at the Rosemary Street Mutual Improvement Association on *Samuel Johnson* and his wife on *Mrs Ewing and her writings*. As well as the building of the new church (see below) Fripp was responsible for various innovations including introducing a monthly church Kalendar.

Rev. Edgar Innes Fripp

Some well known individuals associated with Second congregation

Rev. Edgar Innes Fripp*
(1861–1931)

Edgar Fripp was born in England on 27 November 1861, the ninth child of George Arthur Fripp, a well-known watercolour artist, and Mary (nee Percival). The family were members of Rosslyn Hill Unitarian Chapel in Hampstead, London. He was educated at Milton-Abbas Grammar School Dorset and University College London, where he graduated with a BA degree in 1883. He then went on to study in Manchester College, under Principal James Martineau. He gained a scholarship to study at the University of Jena in Germany. He became a minister in Mansfield Nottinghamshire in 1888. In 1891 he received a call from Second congregation and was installed in December that year. The following year he published a study of *"The composition of the book of Genesis with English text and analysis"*.

In 1900, Fripp returned to England and served as a minister in Mansfield, Clifton, Leicester and Altringham. In 1921, aged 60, he returned to Second congregation where he was formally installed by the Presbytery of Antrim and remained there until 1924. He regularly led a form of liturgical service, which would not be unfamiliar to members of the Church of Ireland. Fripp was fervently anti-sectarian,

> *I glory in antisectarianism. I do not believe that mere intellectual agreement, or mere non-agreement is of much importance. There is something deeper ... man's sense of his need of God, of his sonship of God, and of a divine spirit moving in the soul. It is an emphasis of that which will transform society, and bring about a much larger and deeper brotherhood among men, and completely change most of our social views and class distinctions.*

Following his retirement he devoted himself to the study of Shakespeare and wrote "Shakespeare, Man and Artist". He was made a life-trustee of Stratford from 1925. He died in 1931.

---

* Sources: Haire 1981; Walker 1985; and Rev. John Nelson.

56

ALL SOULS' ELMWOOD AVENUE 1895–1941*

In November 1893 Rev. Fripp suggested that it was time for Second Church to move out of its "decaying property" in Rosemary Street,

I am weary of preaching to empty pews and decaying walls. This place to me is like a tomb. I think I see the hand of death upon it. After working as hard as I, can feel its atmosphere more, not less, depressing. I can look forward to kindness indeed, unfailing, increasing kindness from you individually, but only to certain failure and disappointment in my ministry.

---

* Illustration from an engraving by John Vinycomb M.R.I.A.

57

This suggestion was approved by the church at a special meeting of the congregation on 17 January 1894 and the search began for a new site in south Belfast. Fundraising also began in earnest and within four months over £1,000 had been raised. A three-day Christmas Fair in the Ulster Hall raised a further £800.

The projected budget for building the new church was set at £4,000. However, after competitive tenders were received from construction firms to build a church in Elmwood Avenue to the design of Walter Planck of Beauchamp Road London, the total cost of the successful tender from James Henry of Belfast came to over £6,000.

The congregation also decided that the new church needed a new name. One that was particularly appropriate for a Non-Subscribing church that excluded nobody because of their creed or beliefs. As a result they decided to call it "All Souls'". In Ezekiel it says in God's name "*All Souls are mine*". So for the new church, all men, women and children, nations, sects and parties belong to God and are welcome in the church.

Purchasing the site in Elmwood Avenue and raising enough money to be able to build the new church, enabled the foundation stone to be laid on 25 October 1895, by various local dignatories with connections to Second congregation, including Lady Margaret Montgomery Pirrie, the wife of the world famous shipbuilder Lord Pirrie, who, along with her father, John Carlisle of Queens University, had been a member of the Second congregation. The silver trowel used in laying the foundations is on display in a cabinet in All Souls' church. She was elected an honorary burgess of Belfast (of which her husband had twice been Lord Mayor) in 1904 for her fundraising efforts on behalf of the Royal Victoria Hospital.

As with many building projects, things did not go smoothly. During the building phase the architect suggested various modifications to his plans, which would add significantly to the cost of the building, including a change to the size of the tower. Flowing water, from an old sewer, was also discovered underneath the church, which was later to cause subsidence to the floor. There was a rift between the congregation and the architect, which was eventually resolved by negotiation. The total cost of building the church had now risen to £12,000. The church had only raised £5,000, which was more than they originally thought the total cost was going to be.

A dispute with the First Belfast congregation over the division of the church in Rosemary Street, which was in joint ownership, significantly delayed the sale of Second Church, which eventually raised £6,400. However, despite all the fundraising, the debts owed by Second congregation increased to £3,000 due to the interest to be paid on the loan.

The design of All Souls' was strongly influenced by the style of fourteenth century Anglican churches, which was quite different from the common non-conformist meetinghouse style in Ireland and included a tower similar, if smaller in scale, to that in Crowland Abbey near Grantham in England. The Second Presbyterian congregation moved to its new home in South Belfast in October 1896. The pews from the old meetinghouse in Rosemary Street transferred from the old building to the new. A lead spout-head from 1789 recovered from Rosemary Street was given to the Belfast Museum.

Almost exactly a year after the building work had started, the new church in Elmwood Avenue was completed and opened by the Rev. Joseph Wood of Birmingham who said in his sermon,

> *You have dedicated this beautiful church to what*
> *is universal in religion and in the human heart, by*
> *dedicating it 'All Souls'. These walls are to bear*
> *witness to no sect, no party, no narrow exclusive*

Prayer Book Tradition

With current practice in Non-Subscribing Presbyterian churches in Ireland tending to follow a similar structure to that of church services in mainstream Presbyterian churches, with prayer being extemporised, there is an assumption that this has always been so. However, the history of worship in Second (as well as First) congregation tells a different story.

In January 1893 Second congregation adopted a new worship service book, developed by Rev. Fripp, in the style of the original Church of England Book of Common Prayer, including prayers, responses, psalms, a litany, commandments and beatitudes, drawing on a set of ten services developed by his old Principal, Rev. Martineau. The prayer book was entitled "*A Form of Morning and Evening Prayer together with responses, litany, psalter and collects*". The monthly Kalendar highlighted which parts of the liturgy e.g. Te Deum, Benedictus, Nunc Demitus, Jubilate, etc. would be used in each service. The congregation knelt for prayers. After the move to All Souls' in Elmwood Avenue, Fripp wrote a series of articles in the *Seed Grower* extolling the virtues of most parts of the ancient *Book of Common Prayer* for use by the Free Churches.

This was not the first book of services to be used by Second congregation. Twenty-five years earlier, in 1868, a book of services had been introduced into worship by Rev. Porter and had continued to be used until it was replaced by the new one developed by Rev. Fripp. This followed a tradition begun in 1774 by Essex Street Chapel, London of using an adapted version of Church of England liturgies

Rev. James Street, who was minister from 1871 to 1890, also used a formal book of worship services. Originally this was the book known as the "*Old Ten Services*" (probably the *Common Prayer for Christian Worship* prepared by Dr Sadler and Dr Martineau, published in 1862) and then the revised Edition entitled "*Ten Services of Public Worship*". In 1889 musical arrangements for the "*Responses of the Ten Services of Common Prayer*" were published so other churches could use them.

These formal liturgical forms of service continued to be used in Second congregation well into the twentieth century.

In 1905 when a church correspondent attended a church service conducted by Rev. Drummond, he was surprised that the service "*closely resembled that of the Church of England*". A new book of worship services was then adopted, "*Common prayer in Nine Services*", which had been compiled in England by J M Connell for "Liberal Christian churches in the hope that it may meet the liturgical requirements of their worship", drawing on Martineau's *Ten Services of Public Worship* and the *Church of England Book of Common Prayer*, with any references to the Trinity removed. In 1915 an article in *The Non-Subscribing Presbyterian* said that

> *At all Souls the form is very closely that of the Church of Ireland, with certain minor differences in details due to doctrinal divergences; but the form has the mellow beauty as that of the prayer book service itself.*

When York Street Church was bombed and the congregation and minister joined with the All Souls' congregation in Elmwood Avenue (see below) under Rev. A L Agnew, who used a traditional Presbyterian non-liturgical form of service, the use of any formal prayer book came to an end. This caused some difficulties with the original members of Second congregation who were keen to see the Service Book retained.

First congregation continues to use *Orders of Worship*, containing eight services, plus those for special occasions, compiled in 1944 for use in Unitarian and Free Christian congregations.

Rev A. Elliott Peaston, former minister of the Non-Subscribing Presbyterian Church in Dromore, has highlighted the development of the prayer book tradition, particularly in England in Unitarian and other denominations.

61

creed; they are to speak for ages to come of your
faith in humanity, the faith that endows all that is
human with work and sanctity ... You have
dedicated this church to the faith that overleaps
the barriers of wealth and race, of narrow
convention, social prejudice, and personal dislike ...
keep this church faithful to its great name, to its high
calling, and to its universal mission.

After the completion of the church, work began on the church hall, to be called Rosemary Hall, as a reminder of where they had come from, which was completed in 1908. The congregation were still paying off the debt from the new church and hall for twenty-five years, until 1921.

At the turn of the century, Barrister S Shannon Millin (see profile) wrote a detailed history of the Second congregation in 1900, *History of the Second Congregation of Protestant Dissenters in Belfast*, as well as other pamphlets about poverty, slum housing, and children in the early years of the century. He also wrote two volumes of history about Belfast: *Sidelights on Belfast History*, which was published in 1932.

After serving the Second congregation for ten years, in 1900 Fripp returned to England to be the minister in Mansfield. The Rev. William Hamilton Drummond (see profile), aged 36, the grandson of the Second congregation minister in 1800–1815, became minister of All Souls' (Second congregation). He was ordained for the ministry in 1887 and was minister of North-End Mission in Liverpool, Cross Street Chapel in Manchester and Warrington before coming to Belfast at the end of the century. In 1909 he left Second congregation to become the editor of *The Enquirer*.

Rev. William Hamilton Drummond

Some well known individuals associated with Second congregation

Rev. William Hamilton Drummond*
(1863–1945)

William Hamilton Drummond was the son of James Drummond, Principal of Manchester College and the descendent of the Second congregation minister in 1800–1815. He was born on 1 December 1863 at High Broughton, Manchester and educated at University College London and Manchester College, gaining an MA (Oxon) and Doctorate in Law.

He was ordained in 1887 and was minister of North-End Mission in Liverpool, Cross Street Chapel in Manchester and Warrington before coming to Belfast at the end of the century. He contributed regularly to the *Seed Grower* magazine used by All Souls' and various Free Churches in England. In 1900 he became minister of All Souls' (Second congregation).

In 1907, one of Drummond's Sunday sermons, *The word of God is not bound*, commenting on the New Theology of Rev. R. J. Campbell, was published. In the sermon he demonstrates his commitment to religious freedom,

> *Dogmas decay; creeds die; party cries are forgotten. But the spirit in man is immortal, impelling him ever upward towards clearer vision and nobler goodness. As yet we have grasped but a little of what Christianity is and may become. Fresh light streams forth continually from God's everlasting revelation of Himself. The Gospel of Jesus Christ is rich in prophecy of growth and progress without limits.*

In 1909 he left Second congregation to become the editor of *The Enquirer*. He died on 17 March 1945 in Oxford.

---

* Sources: Millin 1900; Obituaries of Unitarian Ministers (online).

In 1905 Rev. Drummond read a paper written by Dr John Campbell of Second congregation at the AGM of the Association of Irish Non-Subscribing Presbyterian and Free Churches on "The Spirit of the Reformation". In 1907 the congregations of the Association of Irish Non-Subscribing Presbyterian and Free Churches, agreed to unite as one Non-Subscribing Presbyterian Church of Ireland, including the Presbytery of Antrim which Second congregation had rejoined in 1909. Unity was finally achieved by 1910 with the adoption of a short constitution, making the fundamental principle clear that,

> *the teaching of Christ himself must take precedence of the doctrines of a later time, and that unity is to be sought, not in uniformity of creed, but in a common standard of righteousness and obedience to the commandments which Christ himself has laid down.*

The Irish Universities Act of 1908 abolished the old Royal University and granted a University Charter to Queen's University of Belfast, close to All Souls' church, which had previously operated as Queens College.

In 1909 the Rev. Ellison Annesly Voysey (born c. 1867), who had been a minister in Northampton, became minister of All Souls' Elmwood Avenue for only 6 months. He matriculated from Oxford, aged 19, in 1886, where he gained an M.A. He became a minister in 1897. From 1912 he was minister of Dean Row and Styal Wilslow Cheshire. He died in June 1942. His son was a famous architect.

In 1912 Rev. Voysey was succeeded as minister of All Souls' by Rev. Ernest Harold Pickering (born in Leicester in 1881), who had spent two years as assistant to Rev. H Enfield Dowson in Gee Cross near Manchester. He was ordained in All Souls' on 1 October 1912. He had been educated at Oxford and Manchester College. He was a very regular contributor to *The Non-Subscribing Presbyterian* with articles on *"Peace"*; *"Non-Subscription"*; *"A Brief History of our Church"*, based on Dr. John Campbell's History of the Irish Non-Subscribing Presbyterian Church (see below); and *"The Conception of God"*, in which, in 1914, he was still able to say that "No-one doubts that God exists", they just argue about the precise nature of God. He also contributed a regular feature of bible studies for Sunday school teachers. Towards the end of 1914 he spoke at a conference of temperance workers on the relationship between "Drink and Poverty". In a New Year Message in January 1915 in *The Non-Subscribing Presbyterian* he made *"a strong appeal to all the latent Christianity in humanity to arise and put an end, not merely to this war, but to all that which causes war"*. After leaving Second congregation in 1921 he became a Professor of English in Japan and was elected MP in 1931 for Leicester West. He died in Paris on 31 January 1957. In 1910 the Remonstrant Synod and the Presbytery of Antrim (which included Second congregation) merged to form the General Synod of the Non-Subscribing Presbyterian Church of Ireland.

During WWI the Rev. W. H. Drummond, the previous minister, was president of the Belgian Hospital Fund and had toured around the hospitals for wounded Belgian soldiers and on his return gave a talk in Rosemary Hall on what he saw and on what the Fund was trying to do. Of the 28 members of the All Souls' congregation who served in WWI, three (Robert Adair Dickson, Robert McCalmont Pettigrew and Norman Stott) were killed. They are commemorated by a plaque in the church, designed by Rosamund Praegar. Four Duffin sisters served in various military hospitals at home and overseas as Volunteer Auxiliary Nurses. After the war Emma Duffin published a memoir of her experiences in the military hospital in South Belfast. In 1914 Ruth and Celia Duffin published a book of poetry, entitled *The Secret Hill*. Ruth Duffin contributed various stories to *The Non-Subscribing Presbyterian*.

Some well known individuals associated with the York Street congregation

Henry Cassidy Midgley*
(1892–1957)

Harry Midgley was born in Seaview Street north Belfast in 1892. He was educated at Duncairn Gardens school until the age of twelve, when he followed his father into the shipyard. He became interested in labour politics and, having met Keir Hardy, joined the Independent Labour Party.

In the First World War he joined the army and fought on the front in France. Out of this experience he published a book of poems, *Thoughts from Flanders*. He was then appointed as an official of the Irish Linenlappers' and Warehouse Workers' Union and became a key player in the Belfast Labour Party. In 1921 he stood unsuccessfully for the Northern Ireland Parliament and for Westminster in 1923 and 1924. He was successful in being elected to Belfast Corporation for the Dock ward in 1925. He was secretary of the Northern Ireland Labour Party in 1923-5 and 1932-8 and chairman in 1938-42. He was elected, as leader of the Party, to the Northern Ireland Parliament in 1933-8 for the Dock ward.

Midgley was a prominent supporter of the Republican side in the Spanish Civil war. Unfortunately for him the Catholic Church sided with the Royalists and Midgley lost Catholic support, and his seat in 1938, as a result. He was elected again in Willowfield in east Belfast in the by-election in 1941. The following year, however, having failed to persuade the Northern Ireland Labour Party to adopt a stance in favour of the union, he resigned and the pro-nationalist, Jack Beattie became leader. Midgley then formed the Commonwealth Labour Party in December 1942.

During WW2 he joined the Northern Ireland Government, as Minister for Public Security and later, Minister of Labour. He resigned to fight and retain his seat in 1945. To the horror of his former labour colleagues, he joined the Unionist Party and eventually became Minister of Education, where he raised the school leaving age to fifteen and substantially increased the school building programme. Having taken ill at an Ulster Teachers' Union conference, he died in 1957.

---

* Sources: Devlin 1981; Walker 1985.

In 1914 Dr (later Sir) John Campbell from Templepatrick, a leading Non-Subscribing lay-person and member of Second congregation, who had opened Rosemary Hall, published *A Short History of the Non-Subscribing Presbyterian Church in Ireland*.

In 1915 All Souls' started, what would become, an annual festival, with sacred music that had been performed at the first music festival organised by Edward Bunting in October 1813, a performance of Haydn's Creation and selections from Handel's *Messiah*, as well as talks by Dr John Campbell on *Heroes of our Faith* and S Shannon Millin *The Second Congregation as a Factor in the Social Progress of Belfast*. The second 12-day long festival began on 29 October 1916 and included a conference on Child Welfare; a lecture by F. I. Bigger on *General Customs, Ideas, and Beliefs in Ireland in Old Times*; a special memorial service for those who had fallen in the Great War, which included a talk about the work of the YMCA at the front; and performances of several works by Gounod, one of which included 120 performers. The third All Souls' festival was in October/November 1917 and included Bach's *Cantata for All Souls' Day; Heroes Israel*, with pieces from relevant oratorios and short biographical descriptions; a conference on *Present Day Problems*; a lecture on *How Belfast Grew from a Village to a Great City* by J. S. Munce; *A Day of Saints, Heroes and Martyrs* and Rossini's *Stabat Mater*.

In 1917 the congregation pledged itself to comply with the requirements of the Food Controller and conform to any calls made by the Minister of National Service. With the ending of the war, however, the All Souls' festival was replaced by a *Victory and Peace Concert*, the first half of which was a selection of solos and a quartet. The second half was the performance by an all female cast of a pageant written by Rev. Pickering, *The Coming of Victory and Peace*. With the success of that production, the following

68

year Rev. Pickering wrote a comedy in three acts called, *"The Rival Reformers"*, put on by the Drama Society. Later, under Rev Whitehouse, the drama society put on a series of productions, produced by the minister, including *"Mr Pimm Passes by"* by A A Milne in late 1928 and *"Outward Bound"* by Sutton Vane, a year later.

During the Great War the congregation declined in membership. After the end of the war and the return of so many young men who had served during the war, there was a strong consciousness of the need to address the social problems that faced society. In 1919 Rev. Pickering established a Union of Social Services for "the creation of a proper spirit by means of encouraging practical Christian service, and serious, sympathetic study of the problems requiring solution". He became the first honorary secretary of the Union and appealed for financial and other support. However, by November that year it was clear that things were not going as he had hoped. In an address to the Unity Guild he stated his disappointment in no uncertain terms,

> *At one time we Non-Subscribers could boast that we were pioneers in social work. Acting in accordance with that tradition I have endeavoured to inaugorate a properly organised scheme of social work and find to my dismay that we no longer care about being pioneers ... Your indifference has appalled me.*

On 23 December 1920 the Government of Ireland Act resulted in the partition of Ireland, which would result in a bitter civil war.

Some well known individuals associated with Second congregation

Vere Foster*
(1819–1900)

Vere Henry Louis Foster was born in Copenhagen on 25 April 1819, the third son of Irish aristocrat Sir Augustus John Foster, who was Ambassador in Denmark, and Albinia-Jane (nee Hobart). After a period in Turin Italy, he was educated at Eton and Christ Church Oxford. He entered the diplomatic service in 1842 in which he served for five years, including a period in South America, until he made a dramatic decision to dedicate his life to something he felt would be more worthwhile.

He gave a lecture to the Rosemary Street Mutual Improvement Association, *Incidents of Travel in America*, in which he described, in response to the Irish famine, his decision to give up the diplomatic service and

> *take up my residence in Ireland, in hope of making myself useful by falling in with any practical scheme for giving increased employment to the people and for preventing against a recurrence of similar destitution in the future.*

He arranged and paid for more than 12,000 people in poverty to emigrate to North America and travelled in steerage to learn how to respond better to their needs. He wrote about this experience and described the terrible conditions for these passengers and the brutal treatment they received on the voyage, to a House of Commons Commission. This resulted in improved legal protection for people emigrating.

Foster was deeply concerned about the issue of education and travelled around Ireland to see the terrible state of the schools. In response he gave money to each school. He strongly supported the idea of integrated non-sectarian

* Sources: Newman 1993; McNeill 1971; Millin 1932.

70

schools, but faced church opposition. He was elected first President of the Irish National Teachers Association (now INTO).

In 1864, having studied the various systems that existed for teaching handwriting, he created a copywriting book for use in schools. It was so successful that the sales of the books soon reached four million a year.

He was also a strong advocate for education in art and drawing, supporting the establishment and development of the Belfast School of Art, guaranteeing the salary of the headmaster. He was also an enthusiastic fundraiser for the Royal Hospital.

Despite his apparent wealth, Vere Foster died in poverty in a cheap boarding house in Belfast in December 1900. While he gave away at least £100,000 to others, he lived on only £100 a year himself. The Public Records Office describes him as one of the greatest Irishmen ever.

Rev. William H. Drummond of Second congregation said of Vere Foster that,

He had the sprit of the true and gentle knight. He knew how to do great things quite simply. He was full of high-bred chivalry towards the ignorant and the poor. He gave everything to them, and it made him happy to take Poverty as his bride for the good of men ... The age of heroes and the Saints is not only in the past.

Rev. Fripp returned to Second congregation in 1921 to, again, be minister of All Souls' Elmwood Avenue, after Rev. Pickering had left for an academic post in Japan. Fripp was installed by the Presbytery of Antrim and stayed the three years until his retirement in 1924. Eventually the vacancy was filled in 1926 by the newly ordained Rev. Sydney Paul Whitehouse (born 19 April 1894). He was educated at Harvard in the USA, Manchester College and Belfast and continued his studies at Queens while being minister of Second congregation. He contributed regular articles to *The Non-Subscribing Presbyterian*, including on *Confucian religion, Science and belief in God* and *Life – What is it?*, eventually becoming its editor. He left Second congregation, after ten years service, in 1936 and eventually ended his career as minister of Bournemouth from 1960 where he died in March 1978.

After Rev. Whitehouse moved to England, Rev. William Howard Payne was ordained and became the minister of Second congregation in 1936. He had been educated in University College Swansea. Belfast was his first congregation as a minister. He left Second congregation in 1940, by which time the congregation had declined to only 65 families and were in serious financial difficulties. He died in Porthcawl in April 1961. Without a minister for five years to replace Rev. Payne, by 1945 the Second congregation had dwindled significantly and was by this stage in a very poor financial position.

Some well known individuals associated with Second congregation

Samuel Shannon Millin*
(1864–1947)

Samuel Shannon Millin was born in Belfast in 1864, son of John Millin, a flaxseed and salt merchant. Samuel was educated at the Belfast Academical Institution, which he soon left only to re-enrol two years later; and Queen's University, which followed a similar path, not graduating from his three year course, until eleven years later, in 1892. However by then he had decided to enter law as a profession. He qualified in 1894 and took chambers in Royal Avenue and joined the Northeast circuit. He published his first book, *A Digest of the Reported Decisions of the Superior Courts relating to Petty Sessions in Ireland*. With his father's death he decided to adopt his mother's name, Shannon.

Like his grandfather, who had moved from May Street congregation after hearing Henry Cooke preach on Total Depravity, Millin was a member of the Second Congregation and in 1900 wrote a detailed account of the Congregation. His older brother, Adam, was secretary of the congregation for forty years. Millin married Ella Catherine (nee Morton), daughter of Col. David Morton of Sterling and lived in Helen's Bay in North Down. They had two children, Terence John, born 1903, who became a pioneering surgeon, and Betty, born 1905, who became a school headmistress. In 1907 the family moved to St. Kevin's Park, Daltry Road, Dublin, where he attended the Unitarian Church in St Stephen's Green.

Millin was actively involved in The Statistical Society of Knowledge founded during the Great Famine in Ireland in 1847. It soon developed various offshoots, including the Society for Promoting Scientific Inquiries into Social Reform, the Charity Organisation Committee and the Belfast Social Enquiry Society. Millin became the unofficial historian of the Society and contributed regularly to its proceedings. In February 1909 he read a paper to the Society on *The Duty of the State Towards the pauper Children of Ireland* advocating

---

* Sources: Millin 1900, 1932 and papers to the Statistical Society; Froggatt 2004 & 2005.

prevention of pauperism rather than the kind of relief provided by the poor laws. He urged the removal of all children (5,645 in March 1908) from the "demoralising influence of the workhouse" and the establishment of a Department of Children run by women. In 1914 he presented a paper on *Slums: A Sociological Retrospective of the City of Dublin* highlighting, "*the present deplorable condition of the housing of the poor, with its attendant deplorable consequences*". Historically he argued that when the Established Church controlled the political, religious, social and legal affairs of Ireland the state of the areas around its numerous churches "*were a living lie to the fundamental principles of Christianity*". He argued that "*property has its duties as well as its rights*" and proposed a change in the law to reduce the death rate, criminality and the destruction of children's lives by improving overcrowding and insanitary conditions.

The following year he presented a paper on *Child Life as an National Asset* in which he tackled the issue of child labour. He applauded Daniel O'Connell for championing the interests of children. The rights of children were significantly improved by the Children's Act of 1908, but Millin pointed out that the "*filth of our slum dwellings*" defeated the intentions of the Children's Act and created "*the slaughter of the innocents*". In contrast Millin says, "*every human life is of national importance. Even the child in rags*". He also criticised the "*baby farming of the Foundling hospitals*" and the overcrowding of Belfast schools.

He also lectured on culture, including the famous Belfast Harp Festival and Edward Bunting and on poets including William Hamilton Drummond who had been a minister of Second congregation.

In 1928 Millin moved to Maida Vale in England. In the 1930s he wrote a two-volume history of Belfast, called *Sidelights on Belfast History*. He maintained correspondence with Rev. Agnew, the minister of All Souls'. He died in Inwood, Roehampton, England in February 1947.

**York Street Non-Subscribing Presbyterian Church
before WWII**

75

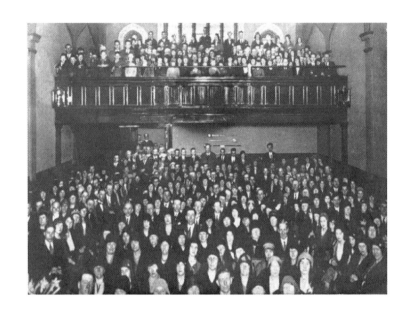

YORK STREET CONGREGATION 1833–1941

During WWII the history of Second Belfast and York Street
Non-Subscribing congregations became intertwined, so we
need to take a brief look back at the history of the York
Street congregation, with its own very distinctive identity.

With the huge increase in the population of Belfast in the
nineteenth century, fed by industrialisation, and the three
Presbyterian Churches all being in Rosemary Street, in
1833 it was proposed to create a new Non-Subscribing
congregation in the north of the city, which had expanded
substantially with working people moving from the country
to work in the mills. At a General Meeting of the Second
congregation on 4 February 1833, the following motion
was passed,

That it is the opinion of this meeting that it would be highly desirable to establish a place of worship where those professing the Unitarian faith may have the opportunity of attending Divine service which is now denied them by want of accommodation in the present houses.

The congregation of First Belfast were approached to support the initiative, but declined. It took another seven years before a meetinghouse in York Street, Beth Birei, which had been built sometime after 1824, was purchased from the Methodists and commenced as a Non-Subscribing Presbyterian church in 1840. Rev. Henry Montgomery, the leading non-subscriber of the period, preached at its opening, stating that the church had *"No pretention to architectural embellishment ... but is substantial, neat and comfortable".*

The first minister of the York Street church was Rev. W. Joseph Blakely, son of the famous Fletcher Blakely of Moneyrea, a leading non-subscriber and tenant right activist. He was installed on 15 December 1840, but died only two years later at the young age of 23.

In 1842 David Maginnis (see profile) became minister of the York Street congregation. Maginnis was well known for his radical theology and the controversy caused by it resulted in York Street congregation leaving the Remonstrant Synod, led by Rev. Henry Montgomery. It joined the much older Presbytery of Antrim, along with Moneyrea, Greyabbey and Ravara, which in itself caused a split within the Presbytery of Antrim over their admittance and the congregations of Larne, Ballyclare, Antrim, Holywood and First Belfast formed the Northern Presbytery of Antrim. Maginnis remained at York Street for nineteen years until 1861.

Some well known individuals associated with the York Street congregation

Rev. David Maginnis*
(1821–1884)

David Maginnis was born near Downpatrick, County Down in 1821. He was educated at Belfast Academical Institution, where he received his theological training under Revs. Henry Montgomery and John Scott Porter. He was licensed by Antrim Presbytery in 1842 and ordained by Bangor Presbytery in York Street congregation in Belfast later that year, becoming their minister aged 21. In 1848 he became the editor of the *Irish Truth Seeker* and was elected Moderator of the Non-Subscribing Remonstrant Synod of Ulster in 1851.

He was heavily influenced by the Trancendalist ideas of Ralph Waldo Emerson and American theologian Theodore Parker, as well as German philosophy and the emerging biblical criticism. Theologically, he wanted to go further than Montgomery. His explanations of Unitarianism caused concern in the Remonstrant Synod and the Presbytery of Antrim. He was accused of "denying the personality of the devil, the pre-existence of Christ, and spoke of Jesus in the same way as Paul or Socrates". He suggested that the students educated by Montgomery and Scott Porter at the Belfast Academical Institution were "half educated and infinitely inferior to those educated in England where biblical criticism was taught". Montgomery called Maginnis and his supporters a "paltry clique" of "wild irresponsible spirits" and was so concerned about the extent of this radical thinking amongst the Non-Subscribing ministers that he attempted to introduce a Code of Discipline with specific questions to be answered by candidates for the ministry, including about the infallibility of the Bible as the Word of God. Despite the opposition of Maginnis and others the majority in the Remonstrant Synod voted in favour of retaining the questions. As a result, York Street congregation decided to transfer from the Remonstrant Synod to the Presbytery of Antrim.

Maginnis was the editor of the *Beth-Berie Magazine* and *The Non Subscriber* from 1858 to 1861. He resigned from York Street in 1861 and was minister in Stourbridge, England until his death in 1884.

---

* Sources: Haire 1981; McMillen; and Rev. John Nelson.

In 1843 Rev John Cordner from Newry was ordained in York Street church by the Non-Subscribing Presbytery of Bangor, not to become minister of York Street, or indeed any church in Ireland, but to go to Montreal Canada, to help establish the first Unitarian Church in Montreal. He was to remain their minister for 35 years.

In 1855 the York Street Non-Subscribing church was rebuilt on the original site. Radical MP Sharman Crawford, supporter of political reform and founder of the Ulster Tenant Right Association, who had made several attempts to introduce a tenant right bill at Westminster, laid the foundation stone of the new church.

In 1862 Rev. John Jellie became the minister of the York Street congregation. Prior to his installation the York Street congregation asked whether it was the intention of the Presbytery to put the three questions contained in the new Code of Practice to Rev. Maginnis' successor. When it was made clear that the three questions would be put to the new minister to be installed, the congregation withdrew from the Remonstrant Synod of Ulster. Jellie had been born in Moneyreagh in 1824 and educated at Belfast Academical Institution. When he was ordained by the Presbytery of Bangor, there were objections to the form of the ordination and the dispute ended in the church court that found by 20 votes to 5 that the ordination had been "unconstitutional, irregular and reprehensible". The ordination was allowed to stand however. He served as minister in Glenarm (1852–1855), Ravara (1855–1859) and Moneyrea (1859–1862). Like Maginnis, Jellie was renowned for his radical theology. He remained at York Street for ten years to 1873. During this period a gallery was added to the church, which indicates that the congregation had increased significantly. He was a strong supporter of the tenant right campaign. At a meeting in the Commercial Hotel Belfast on 29 September 1876 he was elected to speak at a series of tenant right meetings and was later involved in a tenant right meeting in Waring Street Belfast in 1879. He accepted a call to Cairncastle in 1876 where he stayed until he retired from the ministry in 1880 and died on 28 November 1918.

Following the retirement of Rev. Jellie, in 1874 Robert John Orr became the minister of the York Street congregation. Orr had been born in Clonmel, County Tipperary, the son of the Rev. John Orr, minister of Clonmel Non-Subscribing church for almost fifty years. He was educated at Queen's College Cork and Manchester College for his theological training. He became a Unitarian minister in England in 1865. His first ministries were in Bridgewater and Preston in England, before being called to York Street congregation. He stayed at York Street until 1890. He died in September 1915. A display cabinet in All Souls' church has a brass plaque dedicated to the memory of Rev. Orr and Henry J. F. Orr, who died on 14 March 1942.

In 1891 The York Street church was substantially rebuilt to accommodate the expanding population and Rev. Alexander Osborne Ashworth was installed as the minister. He had been born in Rossendale, Lancashire, England on 18 November 1846 and was ordained in 1870. After eighteen years as a minister in England he accepted a call to be the York Street minister in 1888. He remained with York Street congregation until 1909. He died in Belfast on 12 March 1935. In 1910 Rev. John Dare Davies was ordained in York Street and began his ministry there before moving to Clough in 1913 and then to Moneyrea. During WWI there was no minister in York Street and the church faced significant decline. For about six months in 1916 a Baptist minister, Rev. W. G. Anderson, acted as supply minister, but could not arrest the decline. For two months in 1916 the church was closed. After the war was over, in 1919 Rev. Fred Woolley was sent to York Street from the Domestic Mission, where he had been the superintendent, to be the minister.

**Inside York Street Non-Subscribing
Presbyterian Church**

81

In the early 1920s poverty around York Street was severe, with large numbers out of work. Tuberculosis was ever present for working class families. On top of that, the area, which was a major interface between housing mainly for Catholics and housing mainly for Unionists, suffered from extreme sectarian violence, following partition.

By 1923 the number of members of the York Street congregation, which was without a minister, was *"appallingly small"* and some had prophesied that the church would disappear. However that year they appointed a 23-year-old Rev. Arthur Linden Agnew (see profile), often known as "A L", who was born and educated in Northern Ireland, was ordained and became the minister of York Street Non-Subscribing Presbyterian Church in an influential ministry. Within five years the congregation grew from thirty to three-hundred-and-thirty. In September 1926 the congregation began holding an annual service in the Ulster Hall consistently attracting more than two thousand people every year for the following six years. As the York Street congregation again expanded substantially a new gallery had to be added in 1929. Ten years later a gallery was added to the church lecture hall.

The church, despite the economic, social and sectarian problems of the area, again became the hub of the local community. It had social activities every evening of the week, Monday to Friday, as well as Saturdays and two services on a Sunday and a Sunday school. Two plays, *The Haunted House* and *Revolt in Ballyduff*, written by the shipyard poet, Tom Carnduff (see profile) were performed in 1930 by the very active York Street Non-Subscribing Presbyterian Church Dramatic Society.

At the height of his success in York Street Rev. Agnew became seriously ill and in 1928 had to go to convalesce for an extended period, not returning until June the following year, although still not fully recovered and eight months later was forced to again return to Switzerland to try and fully recover. In 1931 Rev Agnew made official visits to Canada, Chicago and Boston, which resulted in return visits from Rev. Preston Bradley of the People's Church in Chicago and Rev. Robert Dexter from Boston. The following year he was again in Boston. He was awarded a Doctor of Divinity from Tufts College Massachusetts. In the 1930s Rev. Agnew also went on an extended visit to Stalin's Russia. On his return he gave talks on Russia on the 23 and 24 September 1936 chaired by Harry Midgley and Prof R. M. Henry of Queens University respectively. During WWII he gave talks to American soldiers to inform them about their ally, Russia.

In 1940 the York Street congregation raised money for a new roof and refurbishment of the church. Unfortunately, not long after the renovations were completed, Belfast was bombed in the early stages of WWII. Despite being a vital industrial production centre for military ships; aircraft; munitions; rope for military use; and tanks, Belfast was described as *"the most unprotected city in the United Kingdom"* and was, therefore, almost completely unprepared, when it was heavily bombed on Easter Tuesday 15/16 April 1941 by 140 German aircraft, dropping 674 bombs and 29,000 incendiaries on North Belfast. York Street Mill was a particular target. 858 people were killed during the raid. Many more were injured. Tens of thousands of people exited the city, sleeping wherever they could. Sleeping in the open in the rural outskirts of Belfast at night and returning home during the day (known as "ditching") continued for many months, until the government threatened to re-allocate empty properties to the thousands of families who had lost their homes in the bombings. North Belfast was bombed again on 4/5 May 1941 involving almost 100,000 incendiaries and 237 tons of high explosives, with a strong concentration on the York Street area, including York Street Mill again. The fire brigade was completely overwhelmed forcing the Unionist Government to ask for help from fire brigades from the neutral Republic of Ireland. York Street church, the hall, including all the church records, Central Hall Rosemary Street and the Domestic Mission, where nine people were killed, as well as many other buildings, including 42 churches, in the area were destroyed or damaged in the bombing, which killed 1,100 people and severely injured 650 others. Half the city's housing was damaged.

One of the things highlighted by the blitz was the terrible poverty in much of working class Belfast. In 1940 the Presbyterian Church commissioned a study, which concluded that one-third of families were in "*considerable economic distress*" and a further 29% were living under conditions which were "*barely sufficient and probably intolerable for any length of time*". In 1941 Dr. Thomas Carnwath carried out an enquiry into the health of the city and named York Street as one of the worst areas.
He described some of the housing as "*mere hovels, with people living in indescribable filth and squalor*", often with "*damp mouldering walls. Many of them bulging, rickety stairs, broken floors [and] crumbling ceilings*". This highlighted the extremely poor record of Belfast Corporation, which unlike in England had built little public housing between the wars. Maternal and infant mortality were 50-60% higher than in Britain.

Maternal mortality increased by 20% between 1922 and 1938. It had also provided only the most minimal health and social services. The Stormont government was similarly complacent. Unionist MP Dr William Lyle, described the facts of infant mortality as the "*slaughter of the innocents*" that "*out-Heroded Herod*" and pleaded for the introduction of a Ministry of Health. The record on education was little better with 93% of children not receiving any secondary education. Following the blitz the York Street congregation was then invited to worship together with the smaller All Souls' congregation in Elmwood Avenue in South Belfast.

84

Well known individuals associated with the York Street congregation

Tom Carnduff*
(1886–1956)
Thomas Carnduff was born on 30 January, 1886 in Sandy Row, Belfast, the son of James Graham Carnduff, an army corporal from Drumbo, who was invalided out of the service, and Jane (nee Bollard). He was educated at Royal Hibernian Military School for four years and then worked as a printer, butcher's delivery boy, light porter, factory hand and catch-boy at the shipyard, before returning to the printing trade, where he worked in the stereotyping department for eight years. In 1914 he started work as a plater's helper in the engine works in the Belfast shipyard, Workman and Clark. He fought with the Royal Engineers in WWI and then returned to work in the shipyard. In 1922 he signed up as a Special Constable with the Special Constabulary North West Brigade. After being laid off by the shipyard in 1938 he then worked as a binman. During WWII he was a civil defence worker. At the end of his career he worked as a caretaker at the Linenhall Library. He was a member of the Independent Orange Lodge, which tried to distance itself from sectarian politics and the wealthy conservative unionists, who dominated the Orange Order.

From the 1920s on he was a poet and playwright and became known as the "Island Poet" (from Queen's island in the shipyard). He had his collection of poetry, *Poverty Street and other poems*, published in 1921, followed by *Songs from the Shipyard* in 1924 and *Songs of an out of work* in 1932. He wrote a number of plays, including *Politics* first performed in 1929; *Castlereagh* about the 1798 rising, published in 1934; *Traitors* performed at the Empire Theatre Belfast in 1934; *Workers*, which was premiered in the Abbey Theatre in 1932; and *The Stars Foretell* performed in Belfast and the Abbey in 1938. In 1936 he formed the young Ulster Society with Denis Ireland and Jack Hayward.

He died on 17 April 1956. An obituary was published by Rev. Agnew. A collection of his poetry and prose was published as *Life and Writings of Thomas Carnduff*, edited by John Gray, based on attempts by Carnduff to write an autobiography and published by Lagan Press in 1994.

---

* Sources: Gray 1994; Craig 1999; Smyth 1992.

85

York Street Church after the Blitz in 1941

ALL SOULS' (SECOND & YORK STREET CONGREGATIONS) 1941–2008

Rev. A. L. Agnew's ministry to the congregation continued after York Street church was destroyed and the working class congregation moved in with the small and more middle class Second congregation in Elmwood Avenue, which was not without its difficulties, including about the nature of the services (see the special feature on the Prayer Book). A few of the surviving York Street artefacts were moved to All Souls' including the notice board outside the York Street church, which contained the following,

> *Membership involves no subscription to any creed. It is open to all who want to worship God and follow Christ in their own way and who value reverent freedom of thought.*

Inside All Souls' Church

87

Rev. Dr. Arthur Linden Agnew

Some well known individuals associated with Second congregation

Rev Dr. A L Agnew*
(1896–1977)

Arthur Linden Agnew was born in 1896, the eldest son of William J Agnew JP, of Moira. He was educated at Moira National School, Lurgan College and Queen's University Belfast. His university education was interrupted by war service with the Royal Naval Air Force 1916–19. Afterwards he returned to his studies and received a BA degree in 1920. He then trained for the ministry at Assembly's College and Manchester College. He was ordained in 1923 and installed in York Street Church.

He had a strong labour congregation and with The Independent Labour Party across the road from the Church, encouraged various left wing groups to meet in the church hall. He supported Harry Midgley (see profile), a labour activist when he stood for the Northern Ireland Labour Party in the 1924 General Election. In 1925 he wrote in *The Labour Opposition* that Christianity and Socialism were the same thing and that Christians should be *"concerned more with present day matters: Housing, education, wages and peace, than with the past doings of the Prince of Orange or the future policies of the Pope of Rome"*. He came into conflict with the fire and brimstone preacher W. P. Nicholson and challenged him to a public debate, but Nicholson refused. Agnew advertised his sermon for the following Sunday, *"Christ or Nicholson?"*

Agnew loved to travel and visited Russia. He also visited the USA on various occasions, where he developed a relationship with the inspirational Rev. Preston Bradley, of the liberal People's Church of Chicago, who also made return visits to Northern Ireland.

After the blitz on Belfast in WW2 the York Street congregation moved to All Souls' in Elmwood Avenue, where Agnew was formally installed in 1944. He was elected moderator of the Non-Subscribing Presbyterian Church for two periods, 1935-7 and 1975/6. Like his father he became a JP and was awarded an OBE. He died on 27 January 1977. His wife Isobel (nee Calwell), who was a doctor, died in 1988.

---

* Sources: Walker 1985; Boyd 1999; Notes from Rev. John Nelson; *The Non-Subscribing Presbyterian.*

Three years later, in 1944, the congregations of York Street and All Souls' agreed to operate as one church rather than seek a replacement for the York Street church, with some dissention from members of both congregations. Rev. Agnew became the minister of the two congregations. The York Street congregation eventually received £7,000 from the War Damage Commission to compensate them for the loss of their York Street Church. So, at this point, the stories of Second congregation and York Street combine to become part of the same story. In 1947 it was agreed that women would be able to become members of the church committee. In July of the same year the BBC broadcast a service from All Souls'.

On Rev. Agnew's 25th year as minister in 1948 there was a special celebration in the Orpheus Restaurant in York Street with 500 people attending. The congregation had commissioned a portrait of Agnew by the famous artist, Maurice Wilks, for the occasion.

In 1955 All Souls', with First congregation, hosted the International Congress of Religious Liberty. Guests attending included the British Home Secretary. The same year gas heating was installed in the church. The Anniversary service attracted 1,200 in the church and hall. Some were unable to gain admittance.

The 1950s saw a strong trend of people moving out of the city to the suburbs, which Rev. Agnew described as a "silent Blitz", potentially affecting the ability of All Souls, with an already scattered congregation, to maintain membership, attendance and social interaction between members. However, in 1954 the annual report records a "considerable increase in membership". In 1956 Rev. Agnew said that All Souls' had the "largest congregation in the United Kingdom" (a claim he repeated in 1971).

There was a wide range of social activities in the church: table tennis club, football club, scouts, a women's guild, men's club, young people's club, bowling club, social hour, Sunday school and dramatic society, which put on *Killybuck* and a version of *Macbeth* adapted by Rev. Agnew. They built an extra room onto the side of Rosemary Hall. Agnew described 1957 as "the best year in the history of the church". The annual report reported ominously "television has become popular". Even the church bought one.

Also in the 1950s Isobel Clements, a member of All Souls' broke a series of long-distance cycling records including four Northern Irish cycling records and four Irish records. The significance of these achievements was highlighted when one of these records, a cycle from Cork to Fair Head (386 miles) was only broken for the first time by a cyclist from Zimbabwe in 2007. The strong relationship between All Souls' and the local cycling club resulted in annual cycling services in the church.

In the 1960s the look of the area in the vicinity of All Souls' changed significantly for the worse. Queen's University, engaging in a fit of outrageous architectural vandalism, decided to demolish an outstandingly beautiful and historic building (The Deaf and Dumb Institute), on the Lisburn Road designed by Charles Lanyon, who had designed the main Queen's University building on University Road, to replace it with the concrete Medical Biology Centre. They also decided to demolish the beautiful Queen's Elms properties opposite the main Lanyon building, which had been used as halls of residence, and replace them with the concrete Students' Union.

Isobel Clements (cycling record holder)

In 1961 Rev. Agnew was seriously ill and had to spend 16 months convalescing in Switzerland. However, the Annual report of 1962 describes it as "*the most successful in our history*". The following year the BBC broadcast a service from All Souls' led by Rev. Agnew, with a sermon about Moses. Two years later he and Rev. John McCleery published *The Story of The Non-Subscribing Presbyterian Church of Ireland – told for its Sunday schools*. Rev. Agnew formally retired in 1966 but agreed to stay on at the request of the congregation.

In 1968, a period of unrest and calls for radical reform in various parts of the world, the civil rights campaign, led initially by People's Democracy, made up primarily of students and lecturers from Queen's University, aimed to achieve improvements in the fairness in housing allocation and voting rights ("one man [sic] one vote"). It began non-violently, but was faced with a violent backlash from sections of the Unionist community. By 1971 it was clear that the Unionist Government was not able to respond sufficiently to the need for reform and the Stormont Parliament was prorogued and the army sent in to protect Catholic communities from attack. Soon appreciation from those Catholic communities turned to anger against armed occupation and an intransigent political establishment and eventually to significant support for armed struggle to achieve a United Ireland.

As increasingly the Second congregation were travelling to the church from further afield there was concern about holding special events because of the civil unrest. Sunday evening services came to an end. The Communion service in Spring 1973 had to be postponed because of the violence. The unrest also encouraged more people, who could do so, to move away from Belfast. In the early 1970s each of the Annual reports refer to the year of the report being the most difficult the congregation had experienced.

In 1971 it was agreed that Rev. Agnew would become the senior minister and the congregation could declare a vacancy and begin the search for a successor. This was to prove a far from easy task, however. There was a special event in 1973 to celebrate the 50th anniversary of Rev. Agnew's ordination. He died less than four years later on 27 January 1977. There was a very large funeral. On 27 March there was a special memorial service conducted by Rev. William McMillan at which the address was given by Rev. Dean H. Hughes.

From January 1977, first Rev Tom Coey and then Rev. Tom Banham were given responsibility for Second congregation, in addition to their other ministerial responsibilities, while the congregation continued to look for a new minister. Several ministers came on trial but didn't work out. The congregation declined in membership and attendance. By January 1982 it was decided to end Sunday evening services because of the low numbers attending. After 12 years without the formal appointment of a minister, in 1989 Rev. A. David G. Steers (see profile) was appointed minister and, despite the challenges involved in following the charismatic, if not particularly democratic, Rev. Agnew and also taking over a church which for a long time had been basically run by the congregation, remained at All Souls' for eleven years.

Various innovations took place during the 1990s including the opening of the church during the month of August (it had been closed in August since WWII); the reintroduction of special Anniversary services on the Sunday closest to All Souls' Day; the introduction of a special annual Christmas Day service; and holding Wednesday lunchtime services, with visiting preachers. The first series of these talks were published as "*A Free Faith*".

Along with other historic buildings of particular architectural or historic interest, All Souls' became part of the Belfast Heritage Open Days, so attracted a significant number of visitors. At night it was attractively floodlit. However, by the late 1980s the stonework of the church began to show serious signs of deterioration and so a major fundraising appeal was launched to raise approximately £80,000 to resurface the stonework in the early 1990s. The church hosted several public meetings of the Presbyterian Historical Society, including a talk on Edward Bunting and the performance of harp music.

Still without a permanent minister the members of the congregation organised special Services of Inspiration in 1993 and 1994, where members shared favourite hymns, poems and readings that inspired them. As this had been such a success, for the Centenary, Lillian Devlin edited a book, "*Wonderful Words*", containing inspirational readings chosen by members of the church and was first used at a special service for the occasion. In the winter on 1994/5 All Souls' hosted a series of Sunday evening conferences to discuss a report compiled by the churches in Ireland on the theme of "*Sectarianism*". In October 1995 a service from All Souls' was broadcast from the church on Radio Ulster. Albert McCartney, who had played the organ at the first radio broadcast from a Non-Subscribing church (Dunmurry), almost fifty years earlier, played the organ for the broadcast. The same month there were a series of Wednesday lunchtime services on the theme of *A Faith to Live by*, and the *Non-Subscribing Presbyterian* published its October issue with a special memoir of the All Souls' congregation by Rev. John Nelson, writing as "Dryasdust".

In 1996 All Souls' celebrated its centenary as a congregation in Elmwood Avenue. It invited ministers, from various traditions, including Father Ambrose McAuley, Rev. John Dunlop, Rev. Henry Keyes and Rev. Nigel Playfair, to preach sermons in the church. The series of sermons was published to celebrate the centenary. A range of other centenary events also took place in the church, including a Festival of Flowers and a concert by the Belfast Philharmonic Choir. Also for the Centenary, Rev. Steers wrote a special booklet about the "*Building of a New Church in Belfast in 1896*", which provides an outline of the background to the church and how it came to be built.

In 2000 the church held a very successful concert to commemorate the first Belfast Musical Festival in 1813, which had been inaugurated by Edward Bunting, the organist of Second congregation. In September of the millennium, a Garden of Remembrance was dedicated at the side of All Soul's Church, including a Memorial Stone upon which the names and dates of deceased members of the congregation could be inscribed, and two gravelled areas, where ashes can be scattered.

All Souls', which has always valued its international links, continued to welcome special guests including Presidents of the Unitarian Universalist Association, Rev John Buehrens and Rev. William F Schulz; Rev. George Stephen, the Moderator of the Presbyterian Church in Sri Lanka; and Rev. Dr Arthur Long, former Principal of Manchester College. The congregation maintained particularly close links with Romania. It had a sister church in Szekelyudvarhely and raised money and sent books to assist in the establishment of an English language school by the Unitarian minister there. Rev. Jozsef Kaszoni, a Unitarian minister from Transylvania, spoke at All Souls'.

Rev Steers left All Souls' in 2000 and has maintained a strong interest in the history of the Non-Subscribing Presbyterian Church (see profile).

Mollie McGeown (Freeland)

Some well known individuals associated with Second congregation

Mollie McGeown (Freeland)*
(1923–2004)

Mary Graham McGeown was born in Lurgan, County Armagh in 1923. She studied medicine at Queens University Belfast and qualified as a doctor. She then gained a doctorate in biochemistry and became a clinical research fellow at the Royal Victoria Hospital. In 1958 she was appointed to set up a dialysis service in response to acute and later chronic renal failure. She was amongst the first to recognise the potential of kidney transplantation and helped transfer the new technique to Belfast, setting up the first transplantation unit in Northern Ireland in 1968. In this unit she developed a unique form of treatment, involving meticulous patient care and anti-rejection drugs, which became known as the "Belfast Recipe", which produced excellent 5-year survival rates. She was responsible for various other important innovations in dialysis, transplantation and nephrology. Her research into renal failure resulted in much greater awareness of the issues and eventually an increase in funding for this area. In 1985 a new transplant unit was opened at Belfast City Hospital, where the renal unit is named after her.

She contributed more than 350 articles for the medical literature, a book on the management of electrolyte disorders as well as contributions to numerous textbooks. She retired in 1988, but continued her work, including editing a book on clinical transplantation and carrying out research, particularly on the long-term outcomes of transplantation. She was president of the Renal Association, the Irish Nephrological Society and the Ulster Medical Society; chair of the UK Transplant Society and a member of the council of the British Transplantation Society. She was awarded a CBE for her services to medicine in 1985 and in 1988 became the first professional fellow in medicine at Queens University Belfast. In 1998, on the fiftieth anniversary of the NHS, she was named as one of the 50 women who had contributed most to its success. Mollie Freeland, as she was known in All Souls', died on 21 November 2004, aged 81. She and her husband, Max Freeland who died in 1982 are commemorated by glass etchings on the windows of Rosemary Hall.

* Sources: Times online obituary.

In 2000 the Non-Subscribing Presbyterian Church in
Ireland issued a Directory of Worship,

> *without putting limitations on the power of the sprit
> it seeks rather to exhibit models which are conceived
> to be agreeable to the simplicity and spirituality of
> New Testament Worship and yet be open to reason
> and a knowledge of the world which God has
> created and put in human charge.*

The Directory provides guidance on: Public Worship and
Private Worship, Acts of Worship and Religious Exercises,
Baptism, The Lord's Supper or Communion, Marriage,
Visits, Funerals, Ordinations, and occasional services.

York Street and All Souls', although technically two
separate congregations, had for all intents and purposes
acted as one congregation for more than fifty years and
finally in February 2001, legally, became a single entity.

In 2006 Rev. Chris Hudson (see profile), from Dublin, was
ordained and became the minister of All Souls', continuing
the Churches historic links with the trade union movement,
through people like Harry Midgley, David and Ruby Purdy
and Bessie Baxter.

An historic watercourse under the All Souls' Church
resulted in subsidence of the floor of the church. In 2007
work eventually began to secure the floor and refurbish the
church with a grant from the Heritage Lottery Fund. During
the refurbishment work, services took place in the church
hall and in the Seventh Day Adventist Church next door. In
May 2008 the refurbishment work was completed and the
congregation were able to return to the church.

Rev. David Steers

Some well known individuals associated with Second Congregation

David Steers*
(Born 1961)
David Steers was born in Liverpool in 1961. He was educated at Liverpool
Blue Coat School (1973–1980) and Christ Church, Oxford where he graduated
with a BA (Hons) 2nd (Modern History) in 1984 and an MA (Oxon) in 1988.
He trained for the ministry at Unitarian College, Manchester and Northern
Federation for Training in Ministry 1985–1988 and obtained his Bachelor of
Divinity from Manchester University. During his studies he was Assistant
Student Pastor at Cross Street Chapel, Manchester (1986–1987). He then was
called as minister of All Souls' in 1989. He was also appointed as Non-
Subscribing chaplain at Queens University and Stranmillis Teacher Training
College.

He has been the Editor of *The Non-Subscribing Presbyterian* magazine since
1993 and a Member of Council of the International Association for Religious
Freedom from 1996 to 2006. He has been a member of Council of the
Presbyterian Historical Society since 1999. He was closely involved in
ecumenical affairs for a number of years serving on the Irish Council of
Churches (1990–1997), the Department of Theological Questions of the Irish
Inter-Church Meeting (1995–1999) and the Irish National Committee of
Christian Aid (1990–1997) and was a founder member of the South Belfast
Clergy Fraternal in 1993 and secretary for some years of the long established
Eclectic Fraternal which brought together clergy from all traditions since the
1940s.

He was also a member of the Council of the IARF (the world's oldest inter-
faith organisation) for 10 years, on the Executive Committee for 4 years and
chaired the European Co-ordinating Committee. He spoke at meetings all over
Europe concerned with reconciliation and religious understanding. In 1997
he led a seminar with Fr Eamonn Stack (who was then working on the
Garvaghy Road, Portadown) on '*The place of dialogue in halting and healing
conflict in Northern Ireland*' at the International Interfaith Centre Conference,
Westminster College, Oxford. He spoke on '*Northern Ireland and Europe*', at
the IARF European Conference, Hilversum, Netherlands, August 1997 and
addressed the Dutch Chapters of the IARF and the World Conference for

Religions and Peace on 'The Churches and the Prospects for Peace in Northern Ireland', Amsterdam, July 2000. He was involved with the establishment of the European Liberal Protestant Network and helped to organise the first ELPN conference at the Evangelische Akademie, Bad Boll, Germany, July 1998. The ELPN brings together liberal Christians from different denominations in Europe. He edited for the ELPN *European Perspectives on Communion*.

During his time at All Souls' he contributed extensively to the literature on Irish non-subscribers and the Non-Subscribing Presbyterian Church. His articles during this period included: *'Religion and Conflict in Northern Ireland*' in Religion and Human Rights in Europe, ed. R. Traer, (IARF, Oxford, 1995); *A Free Faith: Four Addresses Reflecting the Outlook and Ethos of the Non-Subscribing Presbyterian Church of Ireland*, editor and contributor, (Ulster Unitarian Christian Association, Belfast, 1995); *A Handbook for Elders in the Non-Subscribing Presbyterian Church of Ireland*, editor and contributor, (Academic Training Board, Belfast, 1996); *'Building a New Church in Belfast in 1896'*, New Ulster, The Journal of the Ulster Society, No. 30, December 1996; *'Edward Bunting and Belfast's Second Presbyterian Congregation'*, The Bulletin of the Presbyterian Historical Society of Ireland, vol. 25, (1996); *One Hundred Years of Worship and Witness*, editor and contributor, (All Souls'' Church, Belfast, 1997); and contributor to *Remembrance*, eds. G.R.E. Lucy and E. McClure (Ulster Society Publications, Belfast, 1997) and *Cool Britannia? What Britishness means to me*, eds. G.R.E. Lucy and E. McClure (Ulster Society Publications, Belfast, 1999). He continued his studies part-time and achieved an MPhil (Master of Philosophy) with Distinction in 1998 for his thesis on *English Presbyterianism in Lancashire and Cheshire, 1700–c.1830*.

In 2000 he resigned as minister of All Souls' and went to be Dr Williams' Research Scholar and part-time tutor at Glasgow University 2000-3, as well as Chaplain at St Mary's University College. In 2003 he was installed as Minister of Downpatrick, Ballee and Clough Non-Subscribing Presbyterian churches. He has been Moderator of the Presbytery of Antrim on three occasions, 1991/2, 1997/8, and 2004/5.

He has continued to research and write extensively on Unitarianism.

In July 2008 First and Second congregations hosted the conferences of both the International Association of Religious Freedom, at which Rev. Chris Hudson spoke on *"The Liberal Dilemma"*, and the European Liberal Protestant Network.

In 2008 All Souls' celebrated the Tercentenary of the Second congregation.

As of 2008 the Non-Subscribing Church of Ireland has thirty-two congregations on the island of Ireland, all but two of which are in Northern Ireland. There are around four thousand members. It has a close relationship with the General Assembly of Unitarian and Free Churches and is a member of the Irish Council of Churches, the Irish Inter-Church meeting, the European Liberal Protestant Network and the International Association for Religious Freedom.

Rev. Chris Hudson

Some well known individuals associated with Second Congregation

Rev. Christopher Hudson
(Born in 1945)

Chris Hudson was born in Dublin in 1945. His mother, Mary Bridgid (nee Barnes) was a catholic of a mixed marriage from the Holy Land in South Belfast who, because of the troubles in Belfast in the 1920s was forced to move to County Meath. In Dublin she later met Brian "Brackie" Hudson, a builder, who was Catholic, a founder member of Fianna Fail and staunch supporter of de Valera. Chris's paternal grandfather had been an active member of the old IRA, but his identical twin brother had fought for the British in the Boar war as a member of the Royal Irish Fussilers. His aunt, "Molly" (Hyacynth Hudson FMSA), was a nun and his cousin became a priest.

He initially went to a Christian Brothers school, but his father was so outraged by the corporal punishment meted out to his children for being late for school one morning that he removed his children, chased the priest who beat his children and threatened to hang him by his clerical collar. The children were transferred to the Presentation Brothers school. As a teenager he rejected Catholicism and often hung out in the Bamboo Café in Dublin where he became friends with Bob Geldoff. After leaving school at 17, he went to England to work in various jobs, including in a ladies hairdressers, and became involved in the British Communist Party. He spent some time during 1968 in a Communist version of a kibbutz in Czechoslovakia. He left the Communist Party having spoken out against the Soviet invasion of Yugoslavia.

He then decided to return to Ireland and follow his ambition to become an actor, working in the mornings as a postman. He acted in various plays, TV adverts and as a film extra, but turned down the chance to become a full-time actor. He also wrote two plays, which were performed in small theatres. During this period he became actively involved in the anti-apartheid movement and had his first experience of a Unitarian Church in Dublin, with which he felt he could identify.

As a postman he was elected Branch Secretary of the Post and Telecommunications Union in Blackrock and was elected to the National

Executive. Within four years he became a full-time official of the Union, as personal assistant to David Begg. After seven years he became the National Organiser, which he remained for a further seven years. During this period he became involved in the ICTU Third World Committee and from that involvement became active with world development charity Trocaire and then Chair of the newly formed Oxfam Ireland/Northern Ireland.

In 1989 he was invited to join the Peace Train Movement and became joint Chair with writer and broadcaster Sam McAughtry. He was actively engaged in rallies and vigils as well as special Peace Train journeys. The movement also opened books of condolence for people who had been murdered, like those killed in the Warrington bombing.

In 1993, through Shankill Unionist councillor Chris McGimpsey, Hudson met David Ervine at a conference in Dublin, who invited him to the north to speak to a group of UVF members, which he did and developed a relationship of trust, which enabled the UVF to ask him if he would act as a conduit between the UVF and the Government of the Republic of Ireland and opened an important source of dialogue between these leading loyalists and the Government in the Republic, as the IRA had done with the British Government, which helped smooth the way for the the declaration of the UVF ceasefire. He has continued his dialogue with UVF leaders to the present day. In the 1990s he was awarded both the Lord Mayor of Dublin's Award and an MBE.

He became increasingly involved in the Unitarian church in Dublin and trained as a lay pastor. He also undertook a two-year Diploma at the Mater Dei Theological College in Dublin. With extra tuition from Rev. John Nelson he was accepted as a minister of the Non-Subscribing Presbyterian Church and in 2006 was appointed as minister of the All Souls' Non-Subscribing Presbyterian Church in Belfast.

He is married to Isabella Evangelisti, an art historian.

---

* Sources: Mallie & McKittrick 2002; Taylor 1999; Sinnerton 2002; RTE *Would you Believe* March 2007; Belfast Telegraph 1/2/2006; Additional material from Rev Hudson.

THE FUTURE

It is clear that Second congregation has a fascinating and distinctive history. The more important question, however, is what is the future? Over the last fifty years society has been going through the most incredible changes, which are having a powerful affect on people's lives and on those of the churches. Up to the middle of the twentieth century the majority of people still attended church more or less every Sunday, often twice, and for many the church was also the centre of their social life. The relentless advance of secularisation has meant that this is no longer the case. Most churches, including the Non-Subscribing Presbyterian Church of Ireland, have been experiencing falling numbers. The only churches which have managed to resist this trend

Photograph of members of the congregation in discussion outside
All Souls' Church

107

have been the livelier evangelical and fundamentalist churches. So the population has been polarising between those who feel the church is less and less relevant to their lives, and with scientific advances, see orthodox religious beliefs as less and less credible and those who, in a period of rapid change, feel a strong need to cling to a black and white faith, which provides certainties in an uncertain world, and helps try to hold back the tide of scientific and theological development.

Many of those who are uncomfortable with much of traditional orthodox religious faith and no longer feel at home in the churches, still have a strong sense of spirituality and long for ways of searching for meaning in their lives and expressing their own spirituality in a way that maintains their intellectual integrity. The challenge for All Souls' and other liberal or progressive churches, which has a strong intellectual base and is open to scientific insights, is to attract these religious seekers. To do so it must be seen to be relevant to them, to deal with their questions and needs as they are now. The danger for all churches is getting stuck in the ideas, rituals, structures and theology of when they were founded. The Non-Subscribing Church of Ireland needs to keep renewing itself and reflecting a liberal faith in a Twenty-First century context.

All Souls', along with other churches in the Non-Subscribing tradition, has historically played an important and progressive role in highlighting and tackling social issues. The important question is what are some of the key social issues in the Twenty-First Century that the church in Belfast should be responding to? There is no shortage of potential social problems to be addressed, some of which are discussed below.

The Non-Subscribing Presbyterian tradition in Ireland is proud of its openness to those of other religious and political traditions. Many of its members have played significant roles in peace-building and reconciliation.

108

With the Good Friday Agreement and the creation of shared
institutions of government in Northern Ireland, the danger
is that we assume that the problem of sectarianism has been
solved and therefore we can ignore it. If Irish history
teaches us anything it is that if we do not now work hard to
create a culture of trust and understanding and genuine
sharing in housing, education and employment, the conflict
will re-emerge at a later date. We now have the peace to
create a real peace.

Northern Ireland is becoming a more diverse society –
there are now more than two communities. The ceasefires,
globalisation and the enlargement of the EU have resulted
in a significant increase in people coming to Northern
Ireland from other countries. This has highlighted the level
of racism and lack of acceptance of other cultures that
exists (and has been there for a long time in relation to
travellers), and is regularly manifested in verbal and
physical attacks. All Soul's commitment to a liberal
inclusive faith that lays down no specific creed should be
able to play an important role in facilitating communication
and understanding between people of different religions and
cultures. The gay community has also experienced hate
crimes and a feeling of social exclusion, particularly by the
churches. All Souls' should take a lead in responding to
prejudice and discrimination and demonstrating its
commitment to promoting inclusion in practical ways to
these and other excluded groups.

There has undoubtedly been a decline in a sense of
neighbourhood community in our society, against a
backdrop of rapid globalisation. People increasingly feel
isolated from their neighbours, which has an impact on
their feeling of happiness, security and well-being, although
it has partly been replaced by communities of interest and
other forms of social networking. More and more people
see themselves as individuals concerned about their own
well-being, not part of a wider society towards which they
have responsibilities, which can lead to selfishness and a

failure to respond to the needs of others. Increasingly a desire for money and the consumer goods that money can buy are eclipsing values and aspirations rooted in relationships and communities. With the increase in secularism, there has been a decline in participation in and respect for the church and other traditional institutions and a decline in shared values to help guide behaviour, such as tolerance, service and compassion. With the Non-Subscribing tradition of inclusive and compassionate Christianity, which makes no claims for one creed over another, Second congregation has a continuing role to play in helping bridge the lack of understanding and respect that still exists within and between communities in Northern Ireland and rebuilding a sense of concern for others.

Despite increasing wealth in Northern Ireland, the gap between those who are benefiting from increased prosperity, who were mostly insulated from the effects of The Troubles, and those who are unemployed, under-employed, poorly paid, or in unstable employment, has increased significantly. Northern Ireland, like the rest of Britain and Ireland is becoming a more unequal society. There is effective exclusion of around 20% of the population. We also live in a world where we cannot hide from the evidence of huge inequalities and terrible poverty, particularly in sub-Saharan Africa. Issues of injustice and poverty should remain of central concern to churches like All Souls', which has a strong working class and labour tradition. The Bible is very clear about its message about riches and poverty, justice and compassion. There is clearly a need for people who share a belief in a Gospel that calls us to love our enemies as well as our neighbours, regardless of what they think or believe, to stand up and be counted in addressing these pressing difficulties. There is a crucial role for a liberal church with a strong labour and trade union tradition to intelligently translate the message of the Gospel into a powerful force for good in the Twenty-First Century. Fifty years ago few predicted the environmental crisis that is rapidly overtaking the planet. Increasingly theologians have been developing theologies, which reflect a much greater sense of our essential unity with all other living beings and the universe as a whole and our responsibility for effective stewardship of creation. The Non-Subscribing and Unitarian traditions need to reflect this new understanding of our essential oneness, perhaps drawing on Celtic spiritualities, and the need to show a much great stewardship of creation.

There is also the problem of communicating the message of the church to others, most of who will never have heard of the Non-Subscribing Presbyterian tradition. The fact that the name of the denomination is defined by the negative, i.e. "Non-Subscribing", doesn't help either – what is it for? And the name can't be held solely responsible for the difficulties in communicating the message. It is clearly a much wider problem than for All Souls' to deal with, but one that needs to be addressed, to help make it attractive and relevant to a new generation. For most people the concept of Unitarianism is unknown to them and they may not be clear about the relationship between the Non-Subscribing and Unitarian traditions. How the church should confidently brand and communicate itself is a crucial task for the future.

There is also the issue of how to attract people, particularly women, into the ministry. All Souls' has seen the problems caused by long periods without a minister. Perhaps it is an opportunity too, to develop other models of ministry, which give a greater role for lay people in a shared ministry of the people.

Conclusion
Second congregation has much to be proud of. It has played a significant role in the history of Belfast over the last three hundred years. As All Souls' it could also have a very positive future if it is prepared to accept the challenge of

111

responding to the needs of those seeking truth and meaning in a post-modern setting. Those who think deeply about themselves and the society they live in, but no longer find the answers in the traditional language, dogmas and rituals of the mainstream churches. Those who no longer want a church that will tell them what to think and believe. Those who want a church that will accept them as people and allow them to express their doubts and uncertainties, support and challenge them to find a way of being in the world that makes sense to them and enable them to live more meaningful, compassionate and spiritual lives.

I am sure that All Souls' will be able to take up this challenge and grow in size and commitment, so that it has at least as much impact in the next three centuries, as the Second congregation has had in the last three.

REFERENCES

Adair, Lynne and Murphy, Colin (2002) *Untold stories – Protestants in the Republic of Ireland 1922–2002* Liffey Press

Allison, R. S. (1972) *The Seeds of Time – being a short history of the Belfast general and Royal Hospital 1850/1903* Brough Cox and Dunn Belfast

Baillie, W D (1982) *A History of Congregations in the Presbyterian Church in Ireland 1610–1982* Presbyterian Church in Ireland

Bardon, Jonathon (1992) *History of Ulster* (first edition) Blackstaff Press Belfast

Barkley, John M (1986) *Fasti of the General Assembly* Presbyterian Church in Ireland

Blaney, Roger (1996) *Presbyterians and the Irish Language* Ulster Historical Foundation/Ultach Trust

Bradbury, John (2002) *Celebrated Citizens of Belfast* Appletree Press

Brian Barton (1989) *The Blitz – Belfast in the War Years* Blackstaff Press Belfast

Boyd, Andrew (1999) *Fermenting Elements* Donaldson Archives Belfast

Brooke, Peter (1994) *Ulster Presbyterianism* Athol Books Belfast

Bryson, Andrew (1801) *Andrew Bryson's Ordeal* (edited Michael Durey) Cork University Press

Calwell, H G (1973) *The Life and Times of a Voluntary Hospital* Belfast

Calwell, H G (1977) *Andrew Malcolm: physician and historian* Belfast

Campbell, Flann (1991) *The Dissenting Voice* Blackstaff Press Belfast

Clarke, Richard (1997) *The Royal Victoria Hospital, Belfast, A History, 1797–1997* The Blackstaff Press Belfast

Colgan, Brendan (2001) *Vere Foster: English Gentleman, Irish Champion 1819–1900* Fountain Publishing Belfast

Devlin, Paddy (1981) *Yes we have no Bananas* Blackstaff Press Belfast

Froggatt, Peter (2004) *All-Rounders and "Equanimity": Terence John Millin (1903–1980), Irish Urological Surgeon* Ulster Medical Society

Craig, Patricia (ed) (1999) *The Belfast Anthology* The Blackstaff Press Belfast

Froggatt, Peter (2005) *Millin pere et fils: Samuel Shannon (1864–1947), local chronicler* paper read to the Belfast Literary Society on 5 December 2005

Gray, J (ed) (1994) *Life and Works of Thomas Carnduff*, Lagan Press

Haire, J L M (ed) (1981) *Challenge and Conflict* Antrim

Herlihy (ed) (1998) *Propagating the Word of Irish Dissent* Four Courts Press

Hill, Myrtle, Turner, Brian and Dawson, Kenneth (eds) (1998) *1798 Rebelllion in County Down Colourpoint* Newtownards

Holmes, R Finlay G (1985) *Our Irish Presbyterian Heritage* Presbyterian Church in Ireland

Jordan, Alison (undated) *Who Cared? in Victorian and Edwardian Belfast* Institute of Irish Studies Queens University Belfast

Killen, J (1990) *The History of the Linen Hall Library* The Linen Hall Library

Kilroy, Phil (1994) *Protestant Dissent and Controversy in Ireland 1660–1714* Cork University Press

McBride, Ian (1994) *Presbyterians in the Penal Era* Bulletin 27 of the Presbyterian Historic Society of Ireland Copyright University of Notre Dame Press

McBride, Ian R (1998) *Scripture Politics* Clarendon Press Oxford

McCracken (1993) *New Light at the Cape of Good Hope – William Porter the Father of Cape Liberalism* Ulster Historical Foundation

McCreery, Rev. Alexander (1875) *Presbyterian Ministers of Killyleagh*

McMillan, Rev. Willliam *The Non-Subscribers of Ulster in the 18th & 19th Centuries*
McNeill, Mary (1971) *Vere Foster: An Irish Benefactor* London
Malcolm A G (1851) *A History of the General Hospital and other Medical Institutions* Belfast
Malcolm A G (1852) *The Sanitary State of Belfast* Belfast
Mallie, Eamonn and McKittrick, David (2002) *Endgame in Ireland* Coronet Books
Millin, S Shannon (1900) *A History of Second Congregation Belfast*
Millin, S Shannon (1932) *Sidelights on Belfast History*
Millin, S Shannon (1932) *Additional Highlights on Belfast History*
Millin, S Shannon Papers to the Statistical Society: *Our Society: its aims and achievements; Slums: A Sociological Retrospective of the City of Dublin; and Child Life as an National Asset*
Montgomery, H (1925) *Outline of the History of Presbyterianism in Ireland* serialised in The Non-Subscribing Presbyterian
Newman, Kate (1993) *Dictionary of Ulster Biography* Institute of Irish Studies Queens University Belfast
O Snodaigh, Padraig (1995) *Hidden Ulster – Protestants and the Irish language* Lagan Press Belfast
Simms Samuel *40 Notable Citizens of Belfast*
Sinnerton, Henry (2002) *David Ervine* Brandon
Smyth, Denis (1992) *Thomas Carnsduff 1886–1956: Poet of the People* Belfast
Stewart, A T Q (1993) *A Deeper Silence* Blackstaff Press Belfast
Taylor, Peter (1999) *Loyalists* Bloomsbury
Walker, Graham S (1985) *The Politics of Frustration: Harry Midgley and the Failure of Labour in Northern Ireland* Manchester University Press
Witherow, Rev. Thomas (1858) *Historical Sketch of The Presbyterian Church in Ireland* Braid Books & Moyola Books

INDEX OF INDIVIDUALS

Campbell, R J 64
Carlisle, John 58
Carnduff, James Graham 85
Carnduff, Jane (nee Bollard) 85
Carnduff, Mary (nee McIlroy) 85
Carnduff, Susan McCleery (nee McMeekin) 85
Carnduff, Tom **85**
Cartwright, Thomas 4
Castlereagh, Lord 31
Charles II 8–9
Chalmers, John 11
Clements (Woods) Isobel 91–2
Coey, Rev. Tom 94
Connell, J M 61
Cooke, Rev. Henry 39–9, 40, 73
Cordner, Rev. John 79
Courtney, Roger title pages
Crawford (Craford), William 11, 14
Crawford William Sharman 27, 79
Crolly, Rev. William 40
Cromwell, Oliver 8
Cumyng, Dr. Duncan 10
Cunningham, Waddell 21, 44–5
Davies, Rev. John Dare 80
de Valera 105
Dexter, Rev. Robert 83
Dickson, Robert Adair 66
Dickson, Rev. William Steele 36
Donegall, Marquis of 26
Douglass, Frederick 44
Dowson, Rev. H Enfield 65
Drummond, Rev. James 64
Drummond, Rose (nee Hare) 33
Drummond, Dr. William 33
Drummond, Rev. William Hamilton (1778–1865) **31–34**
Drummond, Rev. William Hamilton 61–63, **64**, 65–6, 71, 74
Duffin, Celia 66
Duffin, Emma 66
Duffin, Ruth 66